CELT
MYTHS

CELTIC MYTHS

HEROES, WARRIORS, MYTHS AND MONSTERS

MICHAEL KERRIGAN

This edition first published in 2023

Published by Amber Books Ltd
United House
London N7 9DP
United Kingdom
www.amberbooks.co.uk
Instagram: amberbooksltd
Twitter: @amberbooks
Pinterest: amberbooksltd

ISBN: 978-1-83886-280-0

Project Editor: Michael Spilling
Designer: Zoe Mellors
Picture Research: Terry Forshaw

Printed in United States

CONTENTS

CELTIC PEOPLES

Tales of intrigue and enchantment, of love and war, of feuding families, of honour and disgrace, glory and affliction, Celtic legend has a special quality, at once both immediate and remote.

The Irish said the *Sídhe* were always there, in a realm beyond but immediately adjacent to the world of the everyday, their existence a strange shadowing of, and mystic commentary upon, "real" life. Fairy folk; ancestral spirits; gods, goddesses and ghosts … they were all these things and more – or, maybe, none. So close was their alter-Ireland to the actual country that it was all but constantly impinging, just as their dark and private hillock homes pushed up into the dazzling light of day. Emerging in the dead of night, the *Sídhe* swooped down to kidnap the most promising children to come and live with them, or whisked away the most beautiful women to be their wives. Their goodwill or their jealousy could make or mar a mortal life; their blessing or their curse could define a family's fortunes.

OPPOSITE: **Half-man, half-stag, the fertility god Cernunnos exemplified the mystic closeness the Celts felt with nature.**

At certain "liminal" or threshold times, the two worlds touched, the *Sídhe*'s spiritual presence all but palpable within the reality of everyday. These were moments in which magic might be worked and visions realized, in which imagination and perception coincided. In the glimmering semi-light of sunset or dawn, the sense of another life at hand was overwhelming; in the heady trance of festive tumult, the rules of normality ran all awry. If certain times seemed to belong to the *Sídhe*, so too did certain places – groves and hedgerows, hillsides, streams and ponds: their presence set the landscape shimmering with mystic portent. Writing at the very end of the nineteenth century, the poet William Butler Yeats was to capture the ambiguity of the *Sídhe*'s strange role in the Irish countryside and consciousness, the sense of beguiling beauty and unsettling menace that they brought:

BELOW: Herald of death, a banshee wails above an Irish village, bringing her fateful message from the other world.

Where the wave of moonlight glosses
The dim grey sands with light,
Far off by furthest Rosses
We foot it all the night,
Weaving olden dances
Mingling hands and mingling glances
Till the moon has taken flight;
To and fro we leap
And chase the frothy bubbles,
While the world is full of troubles
And anxious in its sleep ...

Where the wandering water gushes
From the hills above Glen-Car,
In pools among the rushes
That scarce could bathe a star,
We seek for slumbering trout
And whispering in their ears
Give them unquiet dreams;
Leaning softly out
From ferns that drop their tears
Over the young streams...

— "The Stolen Child", 1889

Today in Ireland, a predominantly urban population pursues
prosperity and happiness in a well-established service and
knowledge economy, its besetting problems the usual modern
ones of insecure employment, family breakdown, addiction,
crime ... Today the *Sídhe* belong in stories, strange and stirring:
narratives of the natural and the supernatural – tales of barely
remembered traditions, dream dimensions and spirit lives. Much
of the time it's hard to imagine that anyone ever believed in
such things, such beings as these, as though the existence of the
old myths were a myth itself. Only in the remotest places of the
far-flung west, on moonlit nights beside lost lakes, silent streams
and ominous bogs do we find the faintest intimations of another
life, long disregarded for the most part – but never wholly lost or
forgotten, even now.

ABOVE: **Waves assault
the coast of Dingle Bay
beneath a louring sky.
Did the spirit realm meet
that of humans here?**

Fringe Benefits

What the wild shores of Dingle Bay, the moors of Mayo and
the dunes of Donegal are to Ireland's city-dwellers, Ireland
itself has come to be for continental Europe as a whole. Even in
England, itself an offshore territory, Ireland has been regarded as
remote and in many ways alien. For centuries it seemed a place
of wildness, a place outside. Most of it was literally "beyond
the Pale" – the "Pale" being that area immediately around the

colonial capital at Dublin in which Anglo-Saxon authority had been successfully imposed. Outside that enclosure of orderliness extended a mysterious – and maybe monstrous – territory of ungovernable anarchy, in which a tribal people babbled to one another in a barbaric tongue. What was once a justification for naked colonialism now occasions only the mildest of condescension – but there's still a sense of Ireland as a place apart. A place not only of unruly energy but of lyrical emotion, poetry and song – not to mention mystery and magic. A truly "Celtic" country, in other words.

Much the same might be said of Wales, a nation whose separateness has continued to find cultural expression over 700 years since its brutal conquest by the English. Suppressed but never quite subdued, the Welsh resisted Anglo-Saxon occupation by artistic means – in their language, their bardic poetry, their dance and song. To this day, Welsh nationalism tends to articulate itself more clearly in the cultural sphere than the more explicitly political nationalism of Scotland. That ideological drive in Scotland reflects the modern post-industrial social structures of the cities of the central belt: the country's Gaelic-speaking western Highlands and Islands have a very different

BELOW: **In the mystic light of sunset, standing stones in Spain's Galicia keep Celtic secrets even as they stir the soul.**

feel. Standing on a Hebridean shore in the fading summer twilight, watching as a red sun dips beneath the western ocean, we have the sense of being transported out of today and into an altogether more ancient and enchanted time. We experience the same sensation of existing outside of our present when we sit among the rocks of some far-flung Cornish cove, or pace the silent sand of a secluded beach in Brittany. For France's jagged northwest corner seems in some ways to have

BEYOND THESE COASTS IS ONLY THE ATLANTIC – OR THE ABYSS.

more in common with Wales and Cornwall than with the rest of France; the same goes for Galicia in northwest Spain.

In all these places, the sense we have of being somehow removed from the mainstream of modern life is underlined by literal, geographical remoteness. All these regions and countries occupy the western peripheries of their respective landmasses; all lie along Europe's outer edge. Hence their description collectively as the "Celtic Fringe", and hence too their mystic character, their extraordinary psychogeographical identity. Like the moment in which dawn breaks or the day dies, these mystic coasts seem "liminal": beyond them is only the Atlantic – or, we might as well say, the abyss.

Real People?

Is this too high-flown a way of characterizing a part of the world in which, as in Ireland, ordinary people go about lives that are, in all essentials, indistinguishable from those of the rest of Europe's peoples? True, and true, too, that much of the magic of the Celtic countries has arguably been the "projection" of a modern civilization that desperately wants there to be places that represent an older and less orderly, more romantic, lyrical side. The "Celts" in this sense are a myth themselves, an idea bequeathed to us by generations of our forebears, for whom this race of heroic warriors, wisewomen, poets and lovers embodied ancient values that appeared to have been long since lost. Passionate and authentic, the Celts came to represent the warm, spontaneous "heart" of an approach to existence that too often seemed to be dictated by the cold and calculating "head".

RACE VS CULTURE

The modern study of ethnography emerged in the nineteenth century at a time when it seemed natural to think of different peoples in terms of "race". Different ethnic groups had different characteristics – not just of physical build but of temperament and even faculties; these characteristics were essential aspects of their racial formation. Although it was logical enough as far as it went and stemmed originally from a genuinely scholarly impulse to understand, such thinking resulted in stereotyping at best. (At its worst, of course, it was to legitimize the cruellest atrocities of colonial expansion in Africa, Asia and the Americas and, ultimately, the Nazi Holocaust.) Solid Teutons, strong, steady and organized, were contrasted with passionate but volatile southern Europeans and sensitive and lyrical – but basically unreliable – Celts.

Today, however, it's the whole concept of race whose reliability is questioned: DNA-based research has blown wide open a "science" based on little more than prejudice. The racial identity of the "Celts" has proven particularly contentious: it's by no means clear that the people previously grouped under this ethnic heading really had all that much to do with one another genetically. Indeed, once we think about it for a moment it becomes clear why this would be. Everything archeologists have told us about Celtic society suggest that, elitist to begin with, it was in its pattern of expansion even more so: a chief and his followers imposed themselves on subject peoples wherever they went. The resulting societies were brought together by the attitudes and values the conquerors had carried with them: being "Celtic" had much more to do with culture than with breeding.

Or, more menacingly, in the terms of twentieth-century psychologist Sigmund Freud, the dark and surging secret *id* of unconscious desire only imperfectly covered over and kept in check by the orderly rationality of the conscious *ego*. Hence the ambivalence with which the Celts have traditionally been viewed – an ambivalence that can be traced back all the way to ancient times. Hence too, however, the incomparable immediacy with which their mythology and art always seems to speak to us – as though, alien as it is, it wells up from the innermost recesses of our own souls.

Who were the Celts? And how did they come to acquire this semi-legendary status, this unsettling air of representing our own wilder side? The answer to this question is both complicated and not quite complete – we may never fully understand the ambiguous role that the Celtic myths represent for our modernity. But any sort of explanation must reach right back into ancient times.

A European "Other"

On 18 July 390 BC, a dark day of summer in open country a little way northeast of Rome, the consul Marcus Popilius Laenas addressed his troops. Well-drilled and disciplined, the men who lined up before him as he spoke were seasoned veterans. Through campaign after campaign, they'd honed their skills and forged their courage in their city's endless wars with its neighbouring cities, their efforts bringing the Roman Republic to its present preeminence among the Latin states. This time, however, Laenas warned that things were going to be very different: the danger was of an altogether more disturbing kind. "You are not facing a Latin or a Sabine foe who will become your ally when you have beaten him. We have drawn our swords against wild beasts whose blood we must shed or spill our own."

We can't be certain of the exact words Laenas used – this account was written by the Roman historian Livy four centuries later – but it doesn't seem unlikely that he would have expressed himself in something like these terms. If his comments on the Celts smack distinctly of what today we would call racism, consider what actually happened when his army failed to hold the line.

THE CELTS ATTACKED JUST ABOUT EVERYTHING THAT MADE ROME CIVILIZED.

The Romans routed, the invaders rushed upon their unprotected city and set about a spree of wanton pillage and destruction. To a populace cowering in terror, the last of its soldiers holed up helplessly on the Capitoline Hill, they must indeed have seemed like rampaging wolves. And they didn't just rape and kill: they demolished the monuments that commemorated Roman history and destroyed the documents that recorded it – in short, they attacked just about everything that made Rome civilized.

The savagery of the sack of Rome, and the depth of the Republic's humiliation, seared itself upon the consciousness of the Western world. More than any other event, perhaps, it set the terms in which the Celts would enter the historical records, and that would define their image well

BELOW: **No Roman shrine was too sacred for the Celts to attack, no priest too venerable to be slaughtered.**

into modern times. For the Celts were to be remembered as an untamed, untrammelled "other" in the western psyche – that force for darkness and disorder that seemingly lurked just beneath the orderly surface that so many centuries of civilization, reason and modernity had bequeathed.

That "other-ness" could work both ways, of course: while to some writers of classical times the Celts were unambiguously vicious, uncultured and subhuman, to others (like the famous historian Tacitus) they were admirably independent and indomitable, with a freedom of the spirit that more "civilized" societies had lost. Neither faction made any real attempt to understand the Celts as they might have seen themselves.

WHAT CAN WE REALLY KNOW OF THIS MOST MYSTERIOUS OF PEOPLES?

History, as the cliché has it, is written by the victors, and Roman power was eventually to sweep aside the Celtic cultures across much of Europe. We're constantly – and rightly – reminded of modernity's debt to Rome in everything from architecture and science to politics, law and language. By the same token, though, we've inherited Roman prejudices about what was for several centuries Europe's dominant culture, its contribution arguably every bit as important as that of Rome.

Chronicling the Celts

The Celts might have been better understood if they had left chronicles of their own, but for most of their history they were illiterate – their religion seems actually to have prohibited the use of written script. What, then, can we really know of this most mysterious of European peoples, whose reputation obstructs our view of their reality? Fortunately there is an archeological record that not only furnishes a certain amount of information itself, but offers a critical commentary upon the classical writings, allowing them to be viewed in perspective as genuinely useful, worthwhile sources. Much must still remain unexplained, but between these different records it is possible to piece together at the very least a sketchy outline history of the Celts – a real people, who really did exist.

Alpine Origins

In a bleak ravine, high in the mountains above the Austrian village of Hallstatt, is a salt mine known to have been worked through recorded history. And for quite some time beyond, it seems, as since the eighteenth century modern miners have been turning up prehistoric finds in the twists and turns of its winding tunnels. Quite literally salted away, chemically preserved by the mineral deposits they've lain amongst, have been assorted items left by the men who worked these tunnels almost 3000 years ago. Tasselled leather hats afforded some degree of protection to their heads as they hacked away at the salt seams with picks and mallets, scooped up what they could with flat wood shovels and heaped it into haversacks of hide. Twigs of spruce and pine, bundled into torches, lit their way through this dark labyrinth; bone whistles allowed them to stay in touch with signals. Carrying the salt they'd dug back to the bottom of a central shaft, they would pour it into big wooden buckets that could then be hauled to the surface on ropes of twisted bark. The discovery of utensils and even food remains (again, miraculously conserved) suggest that these miners may frequently have spent considerable periods underground.

ABOVE: A replica of a skeleton excavated at Hallstatt, Austria. The original dated from the sixth century BC.

Researchers estimate that between two and three years' sustained excavation would have been needed even to reach the salt seams from the surface: whoever started this mine had clearly been thinking in the longer term. And it was a large-scale operation: archeologists have identified some 4000m (12,300ft) of prehistoric galleries at Hallstatt, extending 1.6km (almost a mile) into the hillside and reaching a depth of about 300m (1000ft). Yet the entrepreneurs who first established the mine and the industrial community that arose around it are one of the first Celtic communities of whom we know. Archeologists speak of an early-Celtic "Hallstatt" culture.

Iron-Age Advances

It was the acquisition of ironworking skills that allowed Central Europe to undergo its ancient industrial revolution in the early centuries of the first millennium BC. With the help of iron blades, forests could be felled, the earth broken up for cultivation and crops harvested. There were awls and chisels for working wood, hammers and nails for building and iron knives and pots for cooking in constructed homes. The tools invented at this time were so effective that they have for the most part changed very little in the centuries since: most are easily recognizable from those that joiners, carpenters and other craft-workers use today.

BELOW: Enamelled discs and coloured glass adorn this beautifully decorated bronze bracelet.

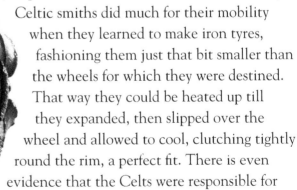

Celtic smiths did much for their mobility when they learned to make iron tyres, fashioning them just that bit smaller than the wheels for which they were destined. That way they could be heated up till they expanded, then slipped over the wheel and allowed to cool, clutching tightly round the rim, a perfect fit. There is even evidence that the Celts were responsible for road building in many of the lands the Romans subsequently conquered: sophisticated roadways, surfaced with tree trunks, have been found. Roman engineers – revered for their road-building skills in modern centuries – may in many cases have done little more than cover Celtic highways over with stone paving. Weaponry was also much improved, especially with the advent of steel, its higher carbon content making for superior strength and durability; iron rings were interlocked to make the first chainmail. The Celts were eager innovators in just about every area of technology, bringing the skills of glassmaking to Central Europe for the first time, and becoming the first people to use the potter's wheel north of the Alps.

A Warrior Elite

These industrious and inventive Celts could hardly be further removed from the romantic stereotype, but this does not mean that the popular assumptions are altogether wrong. Rather, what seems to have happened is that technological and economic advances of this kind in Central Europe underwrote the emergence of a warrior culture. This is where the testimony of ancient historians may come in.

"The Celts are tall of body, with rippling muscles, and white of skin," noted the Greek historian Diodorus Siculus, writing in the first century BC:

"Their hair is blond, and not only naturally so, but they also make it their practice by artificial means to increase the distinguishing colour which nature has given it. For they are always washing their hair in limewater, and they pull it back from the forehead to the top of the head and back to the nape of the neck … Some of them shave the beard but others let it grow a little; and the nobles shave their cheeks, but they let the moustache grow until it covers the mouth."

Their fighting style could be as flamboyant as their appearance, as the Roman writer-general Julius Caesar noted: he had dealings with the Celts in Gaul and then in Britain, which he invaded in 55 BC:

"In chariot fighting the Britons begin by driving all over the field hurling javelins, and generally the terror inspired by the horses and the noise of the wheels is sufficient to throw their opponents' ranks into disorder … By daily training and practice they become so skilled that even on a steep slope they can

ABOVE: Two of the foremost Celtic passions – for fighting and fine craftsmanship – meet in the metal of this splendid shield.

control their horses at full gallop and check and turn them in a moment. They can run along the chariot pole, stand on the yoke and get back into the chariot as quick as lightning."

Diodorus Siculus noted the "individual fashion" in which the "man-sized shields" the Celts carried were decorated: "some of them have projecting bronze animals of fine workmanship", he said.

"On their heads they wear bronze helmets which possess large projecting figures lending the appearance of enormous stature to the wearer. In some cases horns form part of the helmet, while in other cases it is relief figures of the fore parts of birds or quadrupeds."

The commingling of natural and geometric forms in this stunning bracelet typify a Celtic aesthetic that revelled in hybridity.

This account hints not only at the skill of Celtic craftsmen (which was widely admired) but also the way the Celts saw themselves, not as a regimented force, but as individual heroes. Where the Roman legionary's armour was essentially a uniform, marking out his status as a "Roman soldier" and his function within the military machine, the Celtic warrior's proclaimed his personal prestige. The ancient sources have of course to be treated with caution: even when apparently favourable they tend to imply that these "natives" of central and western Europe fought as a brave (or foolhardy) but ultimately undisciplined rabble. On the other hand, the Celts do seem to have had a highly individualistic warrior culture. In that respect, they seemed to hark back to the times of the Homeric heroes rather than the hoplite phalanxes of classical Greece or the highly drilled and coordinated legionaries of Rome – although of course that comparison too may have led classical commentators astray.

ABOVE: Stylized dragons' heads affirm the prowess of the Celtic warrior who wore this golden torc or neck-ring, wonderfully wrought.

Conspicuous Consumption

Status was important to the Celts. As another Greek writer, Posidonius, remarks:

"When a large number feast together they sit around in a circle with the most influential chieftain at the centre, like the leader of a chorus. His position is accorded on whether he surpasses the others in warlike skills, or nobility of his family, or his wealth."

The Celts' love of wine and feasting was notorious, but there was clearly rather more to it than mere gluttony. Banqueting is one of the most obvious ways of advertising power and wealth. Made somewhere in southeastern Europe, but found in Denmark, the "Gundestrup Cauldron" – a masterpiece of Celtic art, ornately worked in silver and holding several gallons of wine – would have made a fitting centrepiece for the richest feast. Another way of impressing people is personal adornment, and this too was an important passion of the Celts, as Diodorus Siculus memorably describes:

"They amass a great amount of gold which is used for ornament not only by the women but by the men. For around their wrists and arms they wear bracelets, around their necks heavy necklaces of solid gold, and huge rings they wear as well, and even corselets of gold. The clothing they wear is striking – shirts which have been dyed and embroidered in various colours, and breeches which they call in their tongue *braccae*; and they wear striped cloaks, fastened by a brooch on the shoulder, heavy for winter wear and light in summer, in which are set checks, close together and of varied hues."

The Celtic taste for luxury is confirmed by the spectacular findings at certain burial sites, where important personages have been buried with mind-boggling quantities of gold. The treasures of the great barrow excavated at Hochdorf, Germany, included exquisite jewellery and daggers dripping with gold together with larger items ranging from a full-sized wagon to a bronze couch and an enormous cauldron. The presumed "princess" of Vix in eastern France was buried with a torc or necklet of gold weighing over a pound (450g), but with detailed animal and other pendants of staggering delicacy. Of rather more interest, perhaps, is the enormous bronze krater or wine-mixing cauldron also found with her, designed to contain some 1250 litres (250 gallons). It, too, is richly decorated – not in the manner of La Tène, however, but with a frieze running round the neck showing warriors, chariots

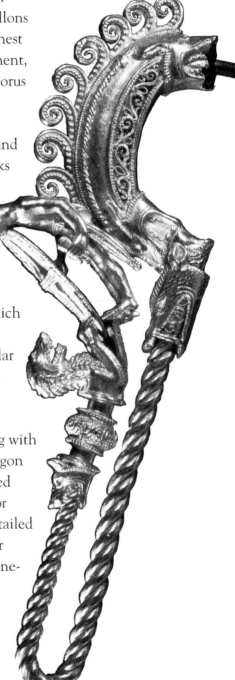

BELOW: **This gold brooch, with its hunting theme, suggests the life of luxury and leisure enjoyed by the Celtic warrior elite.**

and other designs in the Spartan style. Contacts seem to have begun early between the Celts of Central Europe and Greek merchants who traded up the River Rhone from their colony at Massilia (Marseille).

Expansionism

The elite among the Celts who controlled resources – whether mineral deposits, agriculture or overland trade – could thus envisage a life of leisure and conspicuous consumption, punctuated by bouts of heroic warfare. Increasingly, however, as time went on and the population grew it had to be prepared to travel to secure these things. This helps to explain the extraordinary outpouring of Celtic peoples across Europe that seems to have started up at some time towards the end of the Sixth Century BC. The underlying mechanism was straightforward: the Celtic chieftain had to maintain a certain lifestyle to preserve his status, and he had to buy his retainers' loyalty with gifts of cattle, land and luxury goods, hence the need to be conquering, plundering and ultimately settling new territories.

THE SECRET OF THE LAKE

The ornate artistic style that the Celts developed through the middle centuries of the First Millennium BC is known as "La Tène", after a famous lakeside site in southern Switzerland. Here swords, spearheads and other weaponry were recovered from the shallows – apparently tossed there deliberately, perhaps after their owners' deaths. Many are richly ornamented in the unmistakable style familiar to most of us as Celtic – all swirling, spiralling leaves and looping "curvilinear" animal forms. There's no reason to assume that this particular lake was in any sense the centre of what we've come to call the "La Tène Culture" – it just happened to be here that this splendid treasure first came to light in 1857. But the La Tène trove does typify the wonderfully rich and elaborate aesthetic that the Celts were to carry with them across the length and breadth of Europe.

Celtic expansion would quickly take them beyond the immediate Alpine region into southern Germany and eastern France; from there they would spread westward across France and southward into Spain. There, the classical sources say, they first fought but eventually mingled with the native Iberians with whom they created a new and distinctively "Celtiberian" culture. Other groups went over the Alps into northern Italy – including, of course, the raiders who laid waste to Rome. Although never an occupying power, the Celts would remain a presence in the peninsula for well over a century, a sizeable population settling along the valley of the Po. Using these settlements as their base, they seem to have developed a cycle of winter restovers and summer raiding, "commuting" south in spring and returning in the autumn laded down with booty.

During the Fourth Century BC, other groups seem to have moved southward down the Danube valley, settling in what are now Serbia, Hungary and Romania. The collapse of Alexander the Great's Empire after the conqueror's death in 323 BC must have seemed a heaven-sent opportunity for the Celts. Instead

OPPOSITE: Buried with the "princess" of Vix in eastern France, this bronze krater for mixing wine would have made a spectacular centrepiece for any banquet.

BELOW: A Celtic community plans its migration: expansionism was driven by the never-ending need for fresh territories to exploit.

ABOVE: This hilltop settlement at Santa Tecla, Galicia, is one of many to have been found in northwest Spain.

of a strong imperial state, they found themselves facing a leaderless, ramshackle polity, effectively powerless in the face of an attack like theirs. At the same time, however, the Celts in northern Italy were coming under pressure: Rome was no longer a tiny statelet but a mighty military power. Some scholars suggest that this, rather than the vacuum in the Balkans, dislodged the Celts from the land the Romans called "Cisalpine Gaul" – literally Gaul, or land of the Gaels or Celts, this side of the Alps – sending them spilling southeast over Slovenia into the lower Danube. Whatever the explanation, in 279 BC a huge force of Celts suddenly swept down through Thrace and into northern Greece.

The sacking of Delphi and the killing of the priestess there sent out a shockwave to match that produced by the earlier destruction of Rome. The greatness of Greece might lie in the past, but the country still stood for civilization, and the Delphic Oracle was famous far and wide. (And it is fair to say that raids like this did not show the Celts at their most civilized, although reports of their eating babies and drinking their blood are almost certainly exaggerations.) The Greeks were able to turn back the main part of the Celtic advance, but some pushed on as far as the northern shore of the Dardanelles, where they made camp (and where, 2000 years later, their supposed descendants would honour their inheritance in the name of their football team, Galatasaray, of Istanbul). The most adventurous party made the crossing into Asia Minor. Having arrived as raiders, they stayed on as mercenaries for local kings. Some even settled more permanently in the region of north-central Turkey that was subsequently to become known as Galatia – a name that can clearly be seen to be related to both "Celt" and "Gaul". Three centuries later their descendants were to be converted to Christianity by (and receive an Epistle from) St Paul.

To the Margins

That the Celts are now associated with Europe's farthest Atlantic fringes is very much an accident of history: as we've seen, their civilization first arose in the continent's very heart. Indeed, despite

THE GUNDESTRUP CAULDRON

Sounding trumpets, scenes of sacrifice, exquisitely-fashioned animals – and, among other more humanlike figures, the antlered fertility god Cernunnos, a phallic-looking snake in one hand, a vagina-like ring or amulet in the other …. Discovered in a Danish peat bog at the end of the nineteenth century, this stunning silver vessel shows the splendour of Celtic culture – and its scope, not just aesthetic but geographical. Believed by experts to have been made by craftsmen somewhere in southeastern Europe – quite possibly the Balkans – its presence this far north bears striking testimony to the scale of the trade in luxury goods back and forth across the Celtic world. (That the animal figures on the cauldron include what look like leopards, elephants and hyenas suggests that their trading contacts may ultimately have extended even further.) Found buried, with its various component plates stacked carefully upon its base, the cauldron had clearly been dismantled for deliberate interment here, presumably in some time of war or other crisis.

leaving none of the monumental traces the Roman Empire was to, for several centuries it held sway all the way from Iberia to the Balkans. The Celtic tribes were forced to withdraw into the sort of marginal areas they're now associated with by the advance of

THE CELTIC TRIBES WERE FORCED TO WITHDRAW INTO MARGINAL AREAS.

Roman power across Europe as a whole. Julius Caesar described his wars against France's Gauls in considerable detail: he observed their customs too, and their skills in arts and crafts. He called their fortified communities *oppida* – the Roman word for "towns" – and they were indeed considerable centres, the one at Avaricum (Bourges) offering shelter to 40,000 during Caesar's siege. In times of peace they were homes to the nobility, but also to thriving communities of craftsmen and traders, and market centres for the rural communities around. As a soldier, Caesar was interested in the ramparts the Gauls built to defend such settlements, using what he called the *murus gallicus*, the

BELOW: **The Gaulish centre at Avaricum (Bourges) was only captured after a dramatic siege in 52 BC.**

A Babel of Voices

Trying to give a voice to any ancient people is never easy, but for the Celts the task is inevitably more difficult given, first, their own refusal to create any sort of written record and, second, the all but total obliteration of their culture across most of their range. A few little snatches of their speech have been found transcribed into Latin in Roman inscriptions; more often (but much less reliably: the passage of time can be terribly corrupting) they've been memorialized in oral place-name traditions on the ground.

Given how far-flung these ancient Celtic communities were, how local their cultural focus was and how isolated they became through the era of the Roman Empire, it's no surprise to find that they appear to have gradually grown apart linguistically. Modern scholars have identified a number of different Celtic language groups: the earliest, traced back to the Celts' original Central European homeland, is now referred to as Lepontic. In Spain and Portugal, a separate group of languages emerged: these are collectively referred to as Celtiberian – although it's by no means clear how closely this was related to the Gallaecian that was spoken in what is now Galicia. (Cut off from the Castilian heartlands by rugged mountains in an age when a great deal of travel, commerce and communication took place by sea, Galicia didn't belong to Iberia quite as self-evidently as we might now think.) Then there was Gaulish, used in much of modern France and Belgium, western Germany and northern Italy but also ultimately further south and east in an arc from Slovenia to Galatia, Turkey. While the Brittonic language seems to have been spoken – as we might expect – in Britain (England, Wales and Cornwall) and French Brittany, the languages of Scotland, Ireland and the Isle of Man were different again. The tongues that were spoken here belonged to what is now referred to as the Goidelic group: these would not have been readily comprehensible to Brittonic speakers.

"gallic wall". Wooden frameworks were filled with earth and rubble, providing a resilient core that could be clad in a layer of rough stone without and heaped over with soil within.

But substantial as their earthworks were, and heroic as their warriors were known to be, the Gauls could not hold out for long against the Roman war machine. Under the leadership of Vercingetorix, a leader of the Arverni tribe from the Rhone Valley, fierce resistance was offered that came very close to defeating the invaders at one stage. But Caesar's superb soldiers, his tactical brilliance and his sheer good fortune saw him through: the tide was turned and the insurrection brutally put down. In Germany too the Celts were suppressed, an army marching in virtually unopposed in 15 BC. In Spain, the suppression of the so-called Celtiberians had been grotesquely cruel, involving a

ABOVE: **The wild Celt tamed before the regimented Roman ranks: Vercingetorix' surrender to Caesar, as imagined by Henri-Paul Motte (1886).**

succession of sieges and massacres, the most notorious of which was that of Numantia in 134 BC. After a year's indomitable steadfastness, the Celtiberian resistance at last imploded into a spree of cannibalistic violence: even then, the Latin commentator Appian noted in admiration that many chose to kill themselves and their families rather than fall into Roman hands.

Julius Caesar never followed through on his invasion of Britain, in 55 BC, but the Romans returned in the reign of Emperor Claudius in AD 43, and established a hold over all but the far north in the decades that followed. The revolts of Caratacus (AD 47) and the warrior-queen Boudica (AD 60) were more dramatic than militarily realistic. The last stand of the Celtic Picts came at the Battle of Mons Graupius, Scotland, around AD 80, when the Roman general Julius Agricola won a crushing victory.

MANY CHOSE TO KILL THEMSELVES RATHER THAN FALL INTO ROMAN HANDS.

Hence the confinement of the Celtic peoples to the continent's remotest western edges and the marginalization of their traditions in a strongly Latin-based post-Roman culture. Modern civilization, we are constantly reminded, was built on foundations the Romans first set in place – in everything from language to law, from sculpture to town planning. Just as the Celts had been by the Romans, Celtic traditions were pushed aside by a post-Roman cultural consensus maintained down the centuries by Europe's institutions of church and state. Accordingly, a stock of deities and myths was banished to the farthest limits of what was conventionally acceptable, out there on the edge where civilization met the void.

Down the centuries, this literal displacement was to take on a strongly metaphorical force. The Celts acquired a profoundly problematic status in the modern imagination. Real people who live on in legend, their ideas and attitudes utterly alien, their imagery and stories intimately stirring, the Celts came to stand both for our utmost "other" and our innermost selves. It is for this reason, perhaps, that their recollected myths now seem to speak to us so immediately – sometimes so unsettlingly – even when they come to us encumbered by the accretions of later legendary traditions or refracted through the presumptions and prejudices of the Christian scribes who first wrote them down. Important as the myths of Greece and Rome may be in enshrining the founding assumptions of "western culture", this official civilization has always had its darker underbelly, its discontents. Nothing represents that "other side" of life more vividly or compellingly than Celtic legend.

BELOW: Celtiberian tribes were a defining cultural presence across Cantabria, northern Spain, as commemorated by this statue in Santander.

THE CELTIC COSMOS

1

Classical commentators were struck by the centrality of "religious observance" in Celtic life; at the same time they struggled to understand a creed without written scriptures, graven images or constructed shrines.

A mantle of mist shut out the sky above; below, a buffeting wind picked up great squalls of rain and scourged the slopes, their green, scabby grass, their tawny bracken bending to the blast. To the frightened wayfarers watching from the ridge, the hillside seemed quite bleak enough but further down a dismal prospect gave way to one of grotesque revulsion and fear. Covering the valley bottom, curving over like the carapace of a vast and squirming beetle, glossy black shapes jostled and crowded in a hectic throng. A mob of ravens, they draped the ground in deathly black, but, as they frantically pushed and pecked, the viewer caught glimpses of grey, white, gold, bronze and red between their writhing forms. Only by gradual degrees did it

OPPOSITE: The monastery of Clonmacnoise (Cluain Mhic Nóis in Irish, meaning "Meadow of the Sons of Nós") was founded in 544. Celtic art was to become inextricably associated with Christian symbolism – but the early Celts followed a very different creed.

become clear to the dismayed onlookers that this gruesome kaleidoscope of colour represented what had been a battlefield. That mass of mangled mail, of pallid flesh, of gaping wounds, of contorted limbs, was all that remained of the youth of Ulster, cruelly slain.

As for the flapping, croaking, clawing birds climbing over one another in their greed for the broken bodies beneath, there was never any doubt in the viewers' minds of what *they* were. The raven was the emblem (for the want of a better word) of the Morrigan, the war goddess – although it represented her in a way that went well beyond religious symbolism or poetic metaphor. The relation encompassed both those things, though, for the Morrigan was at once a bird and a woman; an imaginative principle and a violent, destructive force. (And, at the same time, a creative one – for death had its place in the cycle of life; dead carrion became living, breeding flesh in the body of the raven, so the Morrigan was also a powerful goddess of fertility and enduring life.) Simultaneously unique and manifold, she could be a single raven tracking its solitary way across the sky above a raging battlefield, a bird of the ultimate ill omen, or – as here – a flock of flesh-eating, bone-stripping scavengers. Numbers don't seem to have signified too much to a cheerfully polytheistic pagan tradition: in some accounts the Morrigan is the Morrigna, a trio (a trinity, even) of bloodthirsty, shape-shifting sisters. Badb, Macha and Nemain too are typically represented as ravens or as carrion crows; again, their names vary according to different local traditions.

BELOW: The Romans didn't begin to understand the druids' religious practices, but they feared their influence over the Celtic Gauls.

Pagan Paradoxes

"The whole nation of the Gauls is greatly devoted to religious observances," Julius Caesar noted – but these observances didn't necessarily have much to do with those of Rome or, still less, our own. Many people in the present day make claims to have espoused a "Celtic" spirituality: the reality is that the day-to-day workings of Celtic religion remain obscure. The multifaceted Morrigan is a case in point: words like "goddess" or "deity" barely begin to do her justice, so complex and so elusive is her essential nature. And she was only one of many scores or even hundreds of other deities, many of whom remain embodied in enduring myths. Hence the importance of the druids or priests who not only knew which gods to placate and by what sacrifices, but when to plant and harvest, and when to hunt. They also had a more social function as doctors, advisors and judges in disputes. The Romans distrusted them severely on this account, seeing them as a source of instability. That Roman writers have been our chief source of information on the druids' activities is decidedly unfortunate, therefore, although one of their most seemingly extravagant charges against these Celtic priests – that they offered human sacrifices at their midnight gatherings – appears to be endorsed by the imagery on the Gundestrup Cauldron.

ABOVE: **Armed warriors parade across one side of the sumptuous Gundestrup Cauldron; to the left a human sacrifice is made.**

WORDS LIKE "GODDESS" OR "DEITY" BARELY DO HER JUSTICE.

The picture is complicated still further for us in the present day by the fact that, if they ever really were a single people, the Celts soon ceased to be as they spread out across Europe, while in later times their hold-out territories were inevitably isolated and far-flung. The Morrigan, for example, is an important figure from Irish legend – although she has her equivalents in the mythic traditions of other Celtic regions. Some 2000 years ago, when our opening scene was set, her origins were already long since lost in antiquity. Her very name was ancient, derived from that same Indo-European tradition in which almost all modern European and near-eastern languages – not just the Celtic ones – find a common root. Its first syllable came recognizably from the word *mer* (or "death" – from which, of course, we get the French word "mort" and the English "mortality"); its second from *reg* (to "lead"; to "rule" – hence "direct" or "reign", the Spanish *rey* or "king" or the French *regime*).

BELOW: **The intricacies of Celtic craftwork are illustrated here on the cover of the Book of Kells.**

Then too there's the fact that in the absence of any written record of their own, the Celts left their oral traditions at the mercy of a posterity that – inevitably – had its own perspectives and its own prejudices. That writing was for centuries the sole property of Christian monks did nothing to clarify the picture: they naturally came at Celtic lore from their own – obviously less than sympathetic – standpoint. To take the Morrigan as our example again, it is ironic that all we know of her has come to us from texts written down by scribes for whom she was nothing more than a monstrous fiction, a scary story.

Let There be Light

It is ironic that a pagan Celtic culture should have found some of its most eloquent expression in a series of carefully crafted Christian texts. For the stunningly colourful illuminated manuscripts made by monks in the religious houses of medieval Europe may be seen as a final (posthumous, even) flowering of the La Tène culture. From early works such as the Lindisfarne Gospels *(see right)* and the Book of Kells through to the high-medieval Books of Hours, the influence of Celtic craftwork can be traced. Those extravagantly ornate colophons, these riotously swirling vegetal patterns and what are now known as "Celtic knots": illuminated manuscripts overflow with ornamentation in the Celtic way.

If, in the person of Christ, according to the Gospel, "the Word was made flesh" (John 1, 14), those same scriptures made words the embodiments of Christ Our Lord. And, to heap one paradox on top of another, the religious

scribes harnessed the aesthetic conventions of a culture that had consciously rejected literacy (and specifically on religious grounds) to help them convey the mystic rapture that they felt in the expression of their faith.

Irish Inclinations

A further fact we need to bear in mind when considering the Celtic inheritance transmitted to us by medieval monks is the bias this has meant towards the heritage of Ireland specifically and, to a lesser extent, that of the Scottish Highlands and Islands and of Wales. For, if the expansion of the Roman Empire had forced the Celts and their distinctive way of life out to Europe's farthest margins, the implosion of that empire in the middle of the first millennium – and the irruption of barbarian invaders that immediately followed this collapse – forced monastic culture to find sanctuary in the wildest corners of the west. Monks took refuge on rock-bound coastal promontories or on the remotest offshore islands where they would be safe – at least until the onset of the Viking raids at the very end of the eighth century.

ABOVE: The Lindisfarne Gospels (c. 700) are a masterwork of Celtic art, a pagan aesthetic pressed into Christian service.

ANIMADVERSIONS

What theological scholars know as "animism" – because it attributes *anima* (the Latin for "life" or "spirit") to many or all natural objects – was once central to most religious belief around the world. Over millennia, it was to make way for the worship of smaller groups of more powerful but consequently more abstract and less locally-rooted deities – like those of Greece (although their association with the heights of Mount Olympus itself suggests an origin in a local cult) or their later equivalents in Rome. Or, centuries later, those of Nordic Asgard. Such systems would in their turn make way for the monotheistic creeds of modernity. (Even then, the Christian notion of the "Holy Trinity" perhaps suggests some vestigial hangover from pagan belief systems – as, still more, may the Roman Catholic veneration of the Virgin Mary and the Saints.) As a matter of simple chronology, then, monotheisms like Judaism, Christianity and Islam are comparatively "modern", whereas animistic religions are associated with earlier, less-developed times or with more "primitive" people. Really, though, from an uncommitted sceptic's point of view, there isn't necessarily any great difference in complexity or sophistication between the systems.

Brennos, the leader of the Celtic warbands that sacked much of central Greece in 279 BC, is said to have been amused to see the statues of divinities displayed in the temples there. To modernity they may represent the height of a classical achievement that is revered as originating that Western culture that holds sway today: to him such straightforwardly anthropomorphic representations of what he saw as much more complex and sophisticated spiritual principles seemed positively primitive, even infantile.

So, while the Celts must have left an important cultural legacy in central Europe, Gaul and Spain, it was only in the offshore islands that the skills and facilities existed for their learning and their literature to be recorded. This book's bias towards the Irish inheritance is, accordingly, in some ways unrepresentative – but it's the inevitable consequence of European history.

A Pagan Poetics

For the Celts, it seems, every stream, wood or valley could have its own proprietary god or goddess – hence, in part, the appeal of paganism to the ecologically-minded mystics of today. There is also its analogous relation to a post-Romantic poetic tradition, which likes to find a quasi-spiritual significance in the beauties of the landscape and of nature. Like Wordsworth's daffodils, Keats' nightingale or Whitman's lilacs, modern literature has approached the natural world in an attitude of wonder not altogether unlike that religious reverence to be found in the paganism of the past. This in itself should warn us of the danger of dismissing Celtic belief as inherently crude, undeveloped or "uncivilized". Like the poet who hears the "babbling" of a brook, the "whispering" of the breeze in the leaves above his head or the voice of a banshee in the howling of a storm, the Celtic pagan looked about and saw a landscape resonating with significance and emotion.

Water wasn't just essential to life; with its fluidity and dynamism it had the character of a living thing itself: every spring was, it seemed, a living spirit. Every bog, its green and shimmering surface concealing a perilous pit of perdition, seemed a treacherous spirit, lying quietly in wait to drag the hapless wayfarer down to a dark and sinister world below. A landmark, a supplier of shelter, shade and fruit, an important tree had its own divinity – so did a lake, a mountain or the warm and friendly (or angry, scorching) sun. It made sense to sum up this character in personified, human terms: hence, the name of the modern-day River Severn, running down the border between England and Wales, clearly comes from the name of the ancient Celtic spirit of the stream, the goddess Sabrina, just as the name of France's present-day River Saône recalls the Gaulish goddess Souconna – and, very likely, that of the Seine Sequana, the presiding spirit of its springs. Ireland's River Boyne is now notoriously associated with a later and in many ways more sinister mythology, as the scene of the battle that saw William of Orange (or "King Billy") establish Protestant ascendancy over a hitherto Catholic country. But it too takes its name from the spirit it seemed to embody to a much earlier, Celtic tradition: the beautiful and regal goddess Boann.

WATER WASN'T JUST ESSENTIAL TO LIFE, IT WAS A LIVING THING ITSELF.

BELOW: **Sabrina, Spirit of the Severn, as imagined by the nineteenth-century English sculptor, Peter Hollins.**

The Poetry of Place

One of the odder glories of Gaelic Irish literature is that genre of poems and prose-pieces known as *dindshenchas* – literally, the word means topography or landscape. These works – of which well over 100 still survive – simultaneously celebrate and set out to explain the origins of Ireland's places: how, first, they came to be, and how they got their names. The name of the River Barrow, which rises in the Slieve Bloom Mountains, Laoise, before running south and west to reach the sea in Co. Waterford, is an anglicized form of the ancient Irish name of *Berba*. This word means "boiling", which, the old *dindshenchas* tells us, is exactly what these normally placid waters did when Dian Cécht, the god of healing, used them to dispose of the burned remains of three monstrous serpents. Fearing for Ireland's future, the Morrigan had given birth to an infant of ferocious aspect – even by her standards – and Dian Cécht had ordered that the boy be murdered for the sake of gods and men. This done, he opened up the child's heart to find the venomous snakes, writhing and hissing as they'd waited to make their escape. Had they been allowed to grow, the god realized, they would have devoured the

BELOW: The peaceful River Barrow shows no sign of the simmering turbulence to which, in Irish myth, it owes its name.

whole population of the country. He killed them, burned their bodies and cast their ashes in the stream. The rest is history – of a fairly fanciful sort, although by no means unusually so for a country whose whole cartography has become a vivid tapestry of myth. "The least Irish place name", wrote the poet John Montague, "can net a world with its associations". This is a landscape into which lyricism and magic are indelibly inscribed.

Fluid Forms

Literally liquid, these deities of water are more widely representative of Celtic belief in their figurative fluidity, their ability to transform themselves in number, shape and form. We find one fascinating example of this outside Saint-Rémy-de-

Provence in the south of France. Thanks to its healing springs, the town of Glanum had been an important Gaulish urban centre or *oppidum* long before the Latin invaders made it a city in the Roman style. Celtic tradition, as reported by the Romans, referred variously to a single (and implicitly masculine) deity, Glanis, and to a trio of divine *matres* (Latin "mothers"), the Glanicae. As we've already seen with the figure of the Morrigan, changeable alike in shape and number, the Celtic deities represented a religion that reflected a world in a state of constant change. Not just the seasons of the agricultural year or the never-ending cycles of day and night (not to mention those of life and death) but the vagaries of the weather – the mists, the wet spells, the sunny intervals, the heatwaves, the droughts, the dearths. Rather than imposing a rigid schema on such things, Celtic spirituality accepted and embraced their transience, finding order in elasticity; eternity in change.

OPPOSITE: Sul, presiding spirit of the spring at Bath, southwestern England, was identified by the Romans with Minerva.

CELTIC SPIRITUALITY FOUND ORDER IN ELASTICITY, ETERNITY IN CHANGE.

In fairness, it should be pointed out that ancient paganism generally seems to have been much more receptive to the idea of change, and to have felt less threatened by transformation and transience. In this respect, it might be argued, it was if anything more sophisticated in its responses than those of later monotheisms that made a fetish out of fixedness and of rigidly regimented order. The word *metamorphosis*, meaning change of form, is Greek in origin, although it was to serve as the title for the Roman writer Ovid's most famous poem. The Romans' organizational obsession is well known: wherever they went they famously built their long, straight roads and carved up the country into manageable units, interspersed with cities built to substantially the same single (and symmetrical) gridiron plan. In matters spiritual, though, they were more open than might be imagined, often as not adopting elements of local belief. Hence their co-option of the Celtic cult of Glanis/Glanicae and, in southwestern England, at what we now know as Bath in Somerset, of the cult of Sul, goddess of the local healing springs. Naming the city they built there Aquae Sulis ("Waters of Sul"), they cheerfully absorbed the "native" goddess into their own religious customs as an aspect of their own existing deity, Minerva, goddess of wisdom. This sort of "syncretism" – the splicing together of figures from otherwise separate traditions – became a pattern the length and breadth of the Roman world. The Gaulish raven-goddess Nantosuelta, closely associated with the healing spring at Mavilly in Burgundy, was taken up by the Romans; her hammer-wielding husband Sucellos identified with Apollo, god of medicine. As a couple they came to represent the complementary qualities of individuals in coupledom, of masculine strength and protection, and of feminine nurture.

A WIDE RANGE OF TREES WERE HELD IN REVERENCE.

Trees and Transformations

One Roman god who, it's thought likely, came from Celtic origins was Silvanus, god of trees and woodland – specifically of hazel groves. The hazel, associated with wisdom, was one of a wide range of trees that were held in reverence by the Celts, both in general, as sacred species, and as individual trees. Of these, the oak is perhaps most famous. To this day it's seen as symbolizing strength and solidity, the augustness of great age and the possibilities of organic growth ("From little acorns …"): the Celts cherished all these same properties. The very word "druid" seems to have shared its roots with the oak tree: the Celtic name for the tree was *dru*. The Galatians were said to have worshipped at a place called Drunemeton ("oak sanctuary").

Even more than the oak, though, the yew represented longevity: not only did it live for centuries, it was evergreen, each year bringing out a new crop of bright red berries. Mistletoe, a parasitic plant that often established itself high up in oak trees, was thought with its milky-coloured berries to represent the promise of fertility. (Hence,

LEFT: **A milk-white bull is sacrificed as a sprig of mistletoe is picked: a Celtic cure for barrenness, it seems.**

presumably, its enduring status as a symbol of amorousness, with all those "kisses under the mistletoe" at Christmas time.) The Roman writer Pliny the Elder described, in his *Natural History*, a Celtic ceremony in which, on the sixth day of the new moon, druids sacrificed two white bulls before cutting mistletoe from an oak tree and making it into a potion to treat barrenness.

OPPOSITE: **Silvanus, Rome's god of woods and trees, is believed to have had Celtic origins.**

METAMORPHOSIS MODERNIZED

In 1899, on the very eve of the twentieth century and at the very threshold of the "Modernist" era in literature, William Butler Yeats published his poem "The Song of Wandering Aengus". In this poem, based closely upon the mythic tradition, an ancient Irish god of youth, of passion and of poetic inspiration describes the distracted state in which he stumbles through his world, conflicting feelings crowding and jostling through his mind:

> I went out to the hazel wood,
> Because a fire was in my head,
> And cut and peeled a hazel wand,
> And hooked a berry to a thread;
> And when white moths were on the wing,
> And moth-like stars were flickering out,
> I dropped the berry in a stream
> And caught a little silver trout.

There's a matter-of-fact monotony about the rhythms of this verse; a straightforward simplicity in its syntactical delivery ("I went … I dropped"); an unembarrassed banality in the repetition of "and … and … and…". At the same time, in its imagery and associations, this poem gets away from its reader, as slippery as its own "little silver trout", as white as chastity, as lithe and determined as a wriggling sperm. Aengus certainly can't control a "catch" that, it turns out, is never more mercurial than when it's seemingly been apprehended. Out of water, this fish is only the more elusive:

> When I had laid it on the floor
> I went to blow the fire a-flame,
> But something rustled on the floor,

(continued opposite)

For the Celts, as for those medieval scribes to whom we owe our modern Biblical narrative of human genesis, the apple was a powerful symbol of life, fertility and growth. On the other hand, there's no sense that the pagan Celts saw it as representing sinful transgression. While its fruit self-evidently stood for fruitfulness, there's no implication that this fertility brought with it any shame. On the contrary, the apple's snow-white blossom seems to have stood for purity and its wood for integrity (it seems frequently to have been used for making wands). The elder tree was sacred too: not only were its white blossom and black berries both used in making sacramental wine, but its very presence was believed to ward off evil and keep human beings and their livestock safe from death and disease. While the ash tree was also held in high regard, the "mountain ash" or rowan was revered still more. A sacred symbol of liminality, it was often deliberately placed outside a house to protect its threshold, but it was also seen as linking the mortal, daily world with the one beyond.

As we saw earlier, the idea of liminality was at the very heart of Celtic imagery and myth – necessarily so, because theirs was a world that could never satisfactorily be encompassed

OPPOSITE: **An endless interplay of intricately fashioned figures, suggesting the ultimate inexhaustibility of life – despite the fact of death – a display of "Celtic knots" adorns an ancient gravestone.**

from one perspective. We see this not only in a body of mythology in which shape-shifting is almost (paradoxically) the only constant, but in the exuberant ornamentation of the Celts' artistic legacy. In addition to a motley host of human, animal and intermediate hybrid forms, La Tène art seems to erupt into flowing, looping lines, to tie itself into "knots" and spirals of stylized vegetal and other forms that swirl around one another *ad infinitum* in a play of – ultimately endless – form. This is not, as later art was to be, an essentially analytical aesthetic in which the divisions between things were marked and boundaries were outlined, so that the nature of things could be defined (literally, "given limits"). Rather, it was one in which the different aspects of existence could be seen to interpenetrate, to co-exist dynamically – even if the sort of "clarity" for which modernity has hankered might not be afforded.

And someone called me by my name:
It had become a glimmering girl
With apple blossom in her hair
Who called me by my name and ran
And faded through the brightening air.

In Yeats's imaginative world, the extravagantly magical becomes mundane; shape-shifting a constant; paradox the norm. The unknown "something" that rustles on the floor is as real and compelling as the "someone" who calls to the poet by his name – but the more apparently real the "glimmering girl" is, the closer she is to fading.

Though I am old with wandering
Through hollow lands and hilly lands,
I will find out where she has gone,
And kiss her lips and take her hands;
And walk among long dappled grass,
And pluck till time and times are done,
The silver apples of the moon,
The golden apples of the sun.

Myth and Modernism went together: the "fire" in Aengus' head suggests the desperate sense of disorientation experienced by those for whom all the scientific and political progress of the nineteenth century seemed in the twentieth to be issuing only in ever deeper intellectual confusion, and in cataclysms of death and war. Yeats was not of course the only thinker to feel this way – or to reach for archetypes out of antique legend. Most famously, Sigmund Freud had seen the dramatic tragedy of the mythic Greek King Oedipus acting itself out in the modern bourgeois family in the son's unacknowledged feelings for his mother and resentment of his father. More generally, beneath the regimented realm of the conscious *ego*, Freud detected a surging *id* of dark and violently disorderly desires of a sort that could only be articulated in the terms of ancient myth.

The Daghda

Despite its localist specificity, Celtic religious practice was by
no means lacking in more general and overarching symmetries
and structures. As we've already seen, similar gods and goddesses
cropped up in comparable contexts across the Celtic world. But
there are deeper correspondences and continuities as well. For
example, it's difficult to resist the conclusion that the masculine
deities appear to have descended from a single common (if often
only hazily delineated) father figure. Of these, the best known
is the Daghda or "good god" of Irish myth. A protective father
for the most part, the Daghda was – like any powerful patriarch
– not to be crossed lightly. Like the Morrigan, the Daghda was a
shape-shifter, appearing in the legends in a number of different

RIGHT: Seen here in the
splendid setting of the
Gundestrup Cauldron,
Taranis was the ancient
Celtic god of thunder.

forms. Most typically, he's a warrior and is represented carrying a fearsome-looking hammer. In some accounts it is a club like that of the Greek god-and-hero Heracles: either way it's a weapon of a particularly potent (and only too obviously phallic) kind. But the patriarchal principle is by no means solely destructive. While, with the head of his hammer, he could kill nine men or more at a single swing, the Daghda could bring the dead back to life with a wave of its wooden shaft. In any case, the "good god" didn't stand only and exclusively for masculine qualities: there were some ways in which he could be said to have transcended sex.

THE "GOOD GOD" DIDN'T STAND ONLY AND EXCLUSIVELY FOR MASCULINE QUALITIES.

Or, perhaps, to have embodied it in all its productive conflicts and contradictions: the cauldron he was often shown with clearly suggested a more womblike and nurturing, feminine side.

The Daghda's hammer is, of course, something he shares with the Nordic deity of thunder, Thor, but the Celts had another god, Taranis (or, in Ireland, Tuireann), in that special role. It was he who set the heavens shaking and sent shafts of lightning down to destroy targets on Earth. His battles with the sun god "Shining" Belenus were believed to cause the cycling succession of dark night and dazzling day. It was to Taranis that the Romans would look when, occupying Celtic countries on the continent, they sought an equivalent for their great god Jupiter, god of the heavens. But the god of thunder never loomed quite so large in the Celtic imagination as Jupiter did in the Roman (or as his predecessor Zeus had done in the belief system of the Greeks). For, as important as the heavens had to be for the Celts, as farmers, travellers, soldiers and seafarers their spirituality was primarily one of the earth, and their fatherly "good god" kept his feet firmly on – or even in – the ground. The Daghda's home, like those of the later *Sídhe*, was generally envisaged as an earthen mound or hillock: on it stood a tree (or a trio of trees), a cauldron and a tethered sow. The tree stooped over, its branches bent with the sheer weight of the fruit it carried, constantly and perpetually; the cauldron was eternally brimming over – whether with inexhaustible supplies of stew or broth or, in more festive contexts, of strong red wine. The plump sow, so suggestive of fertility and abundance, represented that principle of plenty a little more literally as well in the sense that, no matter how many times she was killed and eaten, she was eternally reborn and replenished, a source of everlasting food. Survival and reproduction, still psychologically the most pressing preoccupations of humankind, it might be argued, were for ancient societies much more immediate and obvious concerns. The Celts' chief protector and provider, the "good god" could guarantee life, prosperity and continuing fertility: his favour had to be secured and kept at any cost.

THE CELTS' SPIRITUALITY WAS PRIMARILY ONE OF THE EARTH.

OPPOSITE: A stele from Reims, northeastern France, shows the Celtic god Cernunnos, cross-legged, as he always seems to be.

Mother goddesses abound in Celtic tradition, as they generally have done in ancient agrarian and earth-based cults for which fertility in all its forms has had a central role. That said, it is anachronistic to imagine an opposition between war–masculinity and agriculture/fertility–femininity of the sort we might now envisage. Warfare might have been a man's game in the ancient world, but it was another form of economic productivity, and hence of fecundity – just as the fertility of the soil was seen as the meeting of male seed with "mother" earth. Hence the importance of the cross-legged, antlered god Cernunnos, who in one version or another cropped up all over Gaul, a potent patron of male (and agricultural) fertility. This didn't hold only for the Celts: great Mars himself, Rome's famous god of war, the most obviously masculine of deities, it might be thought, had originally been worshipped as a protector of the people's crops.

BELOW: Epona, Gallic horse-goddess, became patroness of Roman cavalrymen. This charming statue is from Alise-Sainte-Reine in eastern France.

Finding a female counterpart for the Daghda is more difficult, however: no mother goddess seems so obviously pre-eminent as he. Perhaps, paradoxically, because the feminine principle was so important as to be more or less endlessly reaffirmed and repersonified – or was it just that the maternal role was ultimately seen as secondary? The Morrigan, we've seen, could in certain circumstances stand for fertility, but she also represented a great many other, far less nurturing and conventionally "motherly" things as well. How far such seeming inconsistencies would have worried the Celts is unclear: we've already seen how little they invested in rigid systematizations and fixed, established essences – the world and everything in it were fluid and were subject to unceasing change. There was no contradiction, then, between a cruel and warlike Morrigan and her appearance in specific contexts as the gentle, kind and nurturing goddess Anu. (The Paps of Anu, outside Killarney, Kerry, took their name from their fancied resemblance to this goddess' breasts.)

The horse-goddess Epona was protective and kind – although taken up by Celtic cavalrymen in the service of the Romans on account of her equestrian associations, she was eventually to assume a new identity as a military deity. Epona's recruitment into the armed forces wasn't so unusual: Nehalennia, worshipped in Celtic communities along the Netherlands' North Sea coast, seems to have started out as a hunting goddess (hence the hound she was traditionally shown with) but ended up a protectress of Celtic seafarers. In Wales, Dôn and Rhiannon were held in high regard as divine mothers: the former, it has been suggested, was a variant of southwest Ireland's Anu. Or of Danu, of whose existence we can find no direct evidence, even in the mythic tradition, except in the sense that it's implied in the collective name subsequently given to Ireland's ancient gods and goddesses, the *Tuatha Dé Danann*. While the word "Danann", a genitive (possessive) form, has allowed modern scholars to posit the idea of an originating earth-mother Danu, she doesn't actually turn up in person in any ancient tale.

The Heavenly Tribe

Whoever brought them forth, the *Tuatha Dé Danann* seem originally to have been a race of deities – although a later monastic tradition discreetly demoted them to the rank of kings and queens or of fairytale giants, grotesques and witches. Even within the Irish mythological record, accounts of their origins and genealogies disagree considerably, whether because of local variation or retrospective editing by medieval scribes.

AN UNHOLY HOST

Some ancient instinct of appeasement has meant that some of the most unpleasant spirits have the most appealing names: hence the Greek Eumenides or "Kindly Ones" – more accurately referred to as the "Furies". Shakespeare's fairy trickster in *A Midsummer Night's Dream* is called Robin Goodfellow by the same sort of wishful logic that modern Mafiosi were referred to as Goodfellas. It must have been by an analogous process that the *Santa Compaña* ("Holy Company") got its Spanish title, for it is anything but holy in its portent. Its title in Asturian is the more neutral *Güestía* ("Host"); neighbouring Galicia gives it the still-menacing but matter-of-fact title *As da Nuite* – "Those of the Night".

The *As da Nuite* are, basically, a company of souls unfit for salvation and so condemned to wander above the Earth night after night wearing long, white, hooded cowls in a long procession led by a mortal man or woman who's dressed in the same way. This living leader carries a cross or cauldron – reminiscent to a point of the priest's chalice or censer but much more obviously of the cauldron of the Irish Daghda. He or she has been roused from their bed by these troubled spirits but is sleepwalking in some sort of trance and by morning will have no recollection of what he or she has done. The duty is received as a curse – perhaps because a priest has messed up the sacrament of baptism and left the soul without its due protection. The unfortunate victim has to carry his or her symbols of office – the cross or cauldron – at the head of the *Santa Compaña* every single night, and can only offload this duty when the procession meets some hapless wayfarer to whom the sacramental symbols can be handed over.

ABOVE: The *Lia Fáil* or "Stone of Destiny" stands atop the Hill of Tara, in Ireland's Co. Meath.

One thing all the available versions have in common, though, is the sensational, soap-opera quality of the *Tuatha Dé Danann*'s lives and loves. The story of the goddess Boann, whom we've met already, is a case in point. According to legend, this spirit of the River Boyne was married to Nechtan, who is said to have had his home deep inside Carbury Hill in Co. Kildare. Nechtan's name suggests some sort of link to the ancient Indo-European past with that god of water and the sea who was after to be known to the Romans as Neptune – with whom other Celtic water-gods were afterwards to be identified. He, so the story went, presided over his own little well of wisdom in the heart of a hazel grove, its waters filled with enlightenment by nine magic hazelnuts, each of which had fallen into it from one of the surrounding trees. When Boann came to join him in marriage, the enamoured goddess plunged ecstatically into its waters: they overflowed, and so gave birth to the River Boyne.

Boann's passion, apparently too intense to last, ebbed gradually away through the years of marriage until she found herself falling in love – this time with the Daghda himself. Boann fell pregnant and exposure and disgrace seemed to threaten when a desperate Daghda bade the sun to stop in its tracks and cease its circling for nine full months – enough time for Boann to carry and give birth to a baby son, Aengus, who was to grow up a god of youthful beauty, love and poetry. Thanks to the Daghda's intervention, however, time had stood still for the duration of Boann's pregnancy, telescoping the whole process into the length of a single day. No one was the wiser, then, and the infant, fostered out to spare his mother and her lover embarrassment, was brought up by one of the Daghda's more official sons, Midir.

Such shenanigans ran in families: Midir's first wife Fúamnach, furious at being set aside in favour of the younger Étaín, a splendid sun-goddess, turned her rival into a deep well with her rowan wand. But one single change seldom seemed sufficient to the Celtic storyteller: Étaín was successively transformed into a worm and then a butterfly. In this guise she could fly close to her beloved husband and attend him – at least until Fúamnach sent a violent wind that blew her far away, scudding helplessly across the sky for seven whole years. Aengus, recognizing who Étaín was, built the butterfly a bower in which she sheltered for several years, but Fúamnach's fury was by no means sated. Searching high and low, the malevolent sorceress at last succeeded in tracking Étaín down to her hiding place and with another gust sent her hurtling through the air for a further seven years. She landed in a cup of wine that a woman in Ulster was about to drink: nine months later the wife of the warrior Étar went into labour and so Étaín was born for a second time.

Another daughter of the Daghda was Brigid, who in some accounts is considered to be the same person as Boann, but is more widely viewed as

BELOW: **Midir's protective arm couldn't save the lovely Étaín from being changed into a succession of shapes by the jealous Fúamnach.**

one of the most important of Ireland's female deities. A patroness of music, poetry and the arts, she was understandably an inspirational figure for a bardic tradition that would celebrate all three. Her marriage to the thunder-god, Tuireann, might be seen as symbolizing a coming together of brute strength, power, skill and artifice: of their three sons, Creidhne and Goibhniu were both famous smiths, creating masterful works in bronze and silver, while Luchtaine was a wood carver and carpenter to the gods. Much later, Brigid was, of course, to be syncretized into one of the most devoutly revered of Ireland's Christian saints: the chapel St Brigid was traditionally held to have founded in AD 480 was, as its name Kildare (*Cell Dara*, "Church of the Oak") suggests, a place of ancient pagan worship.

RIGHT: **The swirling detail on her carved wooden lectern is here the only hint of the ancient antecedents of St Brigid.**

Wars and Invasions

Unsurprisingly, perhaps, for a warlike people with more than
their share of military expansionism behind them in their
ancestral past, Ireland's Celts viewed their country's history as
a succession of invading waves. One of their most important
chronicles actually bore the title *Lebor Gabála Érenn* – the *Book
of Invasions*. Written up in the eleventh century – so well after
the events it described – and by Christian monks, with their very
particular perspective (which no doubt
distorted things), it still gives a sense of
how Ireland's Celts saw themselves in
relation to their past.

Having essentially rehashed the
Biblical creation story, the writer goes
on to trace a specifically Celtic lineage
all the way from Adam down through
Japheth, one of the sons of Noah.
In the Biblical account, of course,
humanity has grown arrogant and
complacent, and the God of Genesis
sends his famous flood, but Noah
and his family survive. By this time,
however, the story – as seen through
the "mythohistory" of the Celts – has
already grown more complicated: on
the one hand, the line of Japheth
continues through Prince Fénius of
Scythia to his son Nel. On the story
continues, reconnecting with the
scripture with the construction of the
Tower of Babel but adding an exotic
touch with Nel's marriage to Scota, an
Egyptian princess (and ultimately, as
her name suggests, the mother of the
Scots). It is their son Goídel Glas who,
after the collapse of the presumptuous
tower and the division of humanity's
one language into different tongues,

CELTIC GENESIS

In keeping with an aesthetic of ever-
swirling loops and spiralling patterns and a
religious culture of constant and dynamic
metamorphosis, the Celts seem to have lived
'in the moment' philosophically. As rich and
resourceful as their imagination clearly was,
it doesn't seem to have been too analytically
inclined: there's little sign of the modern (or
the classical) rage to pin things down. Rather
than struggling to define, to impose regularity
and order on what they saw, the Celts seem
to have exulted in the complex interplay of
different things.

While Ireland's *dindshenchas* point to an all
but obsessive concern to account for the origins
of those topographical features they found
immediately at hand, less interest is shown in
the question of creation as a whole. This comes
as a surprise to us, as we are accustomed to
think of the 'origin myth' as something that is
fairly fundamental to any culture.

It seems to have surprised those Christian
monks who first wrote down the Celtic myths
as well, so much so that they took matters into
their own hands. In the *Lebor Gabála Érenn*,
what is very obviously a Judaeo-Christian
timeline for the Earth's early generations is
'bolted on' to an existing Celtic chronology
that takes little interest in the creation of
the world.

first speaks the language that posterity will know as Goidelic or Gaelic. His descendants are destined to wander the world for the next 400 years.

Meanwhile, however, in another narrative line, Cessair, the daughter of another of Noah's sons Bith, has already set out – before the great flood – with a party of settlers who eventually find themselves in Ireland. After warnings of the deluge to come, they seek sanctuary in the mountains of the west. Only one, Fintán, survives in a series of different forms – first as a salmon, then as an eagle, then as a hawk. Not until 5000 years later does he finally resume his human shape to become an important chronicler of Irish history.

By that time, several further waves of settlers in Ireland have been and gone: the first of these is the Muíntir Partholón or "people of Partholón". Their leader, Partholón, another descendant of Noah, establishes a successful civilization on the island – but only briefly, as it is quickly swept away by plague.

ABOVE: Fintán, it's said, survived Noah's flood in the form of a salmon, before later becoming an eagle and a hawk.

Not, however, before a mysterious race of would-be invaders, the Fomorians, have been beaten back; or before the skills of agriculture, livestock husbandry, household management and construction have been established. After another 30 years, a new wave of settlers arrives under the leadership of Nemed. He too, it turns out, is descended from the Noah of the Bible. Of the 40-odd ships with which his expedition first departs from western Asia's Caspian Sea, only Nemed's actually makes it through the storms to the western isle. He, his wife, his sons and their supporters set about clearing forests and bringing Ireland under the plough.

They too have to contend with the aggressive attentions of the Fomorians: four times they attack, and four times they are defeated. Finally, however, the raiders, under the leadership of Conand and Morc, succeed in conquering the Nemedians and making them pay tribute. Every summer, at the harvest festival of Samhain, they have to give up two-thirds of their produce – and their children – to the Fomorians.

FOUR TIMES THEY ATTACK, AND FOUR TIMES THEY ARE DEFEATED.

At last, in a fury they attack King Conand in his fortified tower on Tory Island off the Donegal coast, but although they succeed in destroying him, they are crushed in turn by a Fomorian relief-force led by Morc. Those who aren't killed on the battlefield are largely swept away by an enormous ocean swell: the handful who survive are scattered throughout the wider world. While one group goes off to establish Britain to the east and others head off into the north (and, for the time being, into oblivion), a third party sails south for the Aegean sea where they will find sanctuary – of a sort – in Greece. In fact, the founders of western civilization welcome their new arrivals only as slaves. They are

BELOW: Tory Island became the headquarters from which King Conand oppressed the Nemedians – until they rose up and attacked him there.

forced to carry clay in their quarries, packing it into great sacks, hence the name they come to be known by: *Fir Bolg*, or "men of bags". Rebuilding their strength over generations, however, after 230 years they are ready to return to Ireland, still uninhabited since the tsunami two centuries before. Five *Fir Bolg* chieftains disperse themselves, with their families and followers, around the empty island.

Tuatha Takeover

All this time, that group of "Nemedians" who fled north after the defeat by the Fomorians have been holding out in quiet isolation. Now, under their King Nuada, the *Tuatha Dé Danann* are growing rich and strong. Suddenly, and by mysterious – possibly magic – means, for this "people" occupy an ambiguous status somewhere between mortal humans and immortal deities, they reappear in Ireland to take on the *Fir Bolg*. Comparing the different sources on this episode, we can pretty much see the power struggle between a Celtic tradition that sees the *Tuatha Dé Danann* as gods and a Christian revisionism that prefers to see them as human heroes. In some versions they descend in dark clouds atop the Connemara mountains, and from among its mists they magically take form; in others they land on the Connacht coasts like normal raiders.

Either way, the *Tuatha Dé Danann* win the ensuing struggle, although Nuada himself is badly wounded in the fray. In the Battle of Magh Tuireadh, on a plain in the heart of Connacht, he loses his arm, and – no longer physically perfect – is disqualified as king. For the time being he is ousted by Bres, whose lineage and loyalties alike incline him towards an accommodation with the Fomorians – still waiting in the wings. The alliance quickly proves unequal, even though the *Tuatha Dé Danann* have won their recent battles: under what amounts to Fomorian rule, they are reduced to servitude. The Daghda, for instance, is sentenced to spend his days digging ditches, an ignominious fate for the father of the gods. But Nuada has a special silver arm fashioned for him by Dian Cécht, the god of

BELOW: The Daghda's cauldron or undry afforded never-ending abundance – and symbolized a supremely masculine deity's more maternal side.

LUGHNASADH

The honorific Lugh means "long-armed", in tribute to the deity's unparalleled mastery as thrower with spear or sling, although it harks back as well to *leuk*, an Indo-European word meaning "light". It's no great surprise, then, to find that Lugh was strongly associated with the sun, or that his great festival, Lughnasadh, should have come at the climax of the summer at harvest time. Similar festivals were celebrated in Scotland and the Isle of Man – and, it would seem likely, throughout the Celtic world. Lughnasadh was marked by offerings of freshly reaped grain and fruit, and the sacrifice of a bull to thank Lugh for the fertility and plenty he had brought his people. These were typically carried to hilltops that were deemed sacred to the god. The custom of climbing mountains in Lugh's honour is believed to have been reinvented in the Christian era as a penitential pilgrimage, like the long tramp up Croagh Patrick in Co. Mayo each year on the last Sunday in July.

LEFT: Lugh wields his bloodthirsty magic spear.

healing, and is able to assume the leadership of his people once again. Together they rise and, defeating the Fomorians, restore the *Tuatha Dé Danann* to the ascendancy in Ireland.

Down but not yet fully out, the Fomorians come back to reassert their authority, but they're defeated at the Second Battle of Magh Tuireadh. For the *Tuatha Dé Danann* it is to some extent a hollow triumph, for their King Nuada falls in the hour of victory, and as a tribe they feel

TOGETHER THEY RISE AND RESTORE THE TUATHA TO THE ASCENDANCY.

completely lost without him. His successor, Lugh, like Bres, is part-Fomorian by background, but he proves more loyal to the *Tuatha Dé Danann*.

Gael Force

It seems to have been about now that a long-forgotten strand of Celtic history comes back to haunt the Irish – one that takes us all the way back to the fall of Babel. After wandering the earth for some 400 years, the descendants of Goídel Glas had found themselves off the Iberian coast: here one Breogan had set himself up as King of Brigantia (now Galicia) in northwestern Spain. There he built another great tower, from whose top one day his brother Íth caught sight of a green and distant land across

RIGHT: A Celtic descendant of Goídel Glas, Breogan became founder of an important ruling dynasty in northern Spain.

the waves. Breogan's son promptly organized an expeditionary force, assembling his finest warriors to set sail for the island, which they then took from the *Tuatha Dé Danann* by force. The young conqueror's given name isn't clear: the name he's known by, Míl Espaine, is no more than a gaelicization of the Latin *Miles Hispania*, "Soldier of Spain"; his followers and their families have been referred to as "Milesians".

As descendants of Goídel Glas, they were also the first "Gaels" to come to Ireland, giving the country an identity it would retain down to the present day. They were also to establish a new cosmic order, literally driving the defeated *Tuatha Dé Danann* underground. There, these former deities – now reduced to the rank of fairy-folk and mischief-makers – were forced to take up residence, to emerge only at night as the *Sídhe*. As for the Milesians, their status was unclear: for the most part they remained as mortal men and women, although some do seem to have enjoyed divine status of a sort.

Not necessarily of an enviable kind, however: Donn, a son of Míl Espaine, made the mistake of insulting – and, still worse, underestimating – the goddess Ériu. Despite the *Tuatha Dé Danann*'s fall from power above Earth, they still held sway below, and the mother-goddess Ériu was enduringly important enough to have given her name to Eire, or Ireland. Donn, dragged down beneath the waves to drown as he sailed his ship off the southwestern Irish coast, was eternally incarcerated inside a rocky islet off the Beara Peninsula, Co. Cork. Now known as "Bull Rock" (basically because it's bigger than the "Calf Rock", which stands nearby), this figures in the old *dindshenchas* as Tech Duinn (the "House of Donn"). According t o an anonymous poet, the souls of sinners visit Tech Duinn before they go to hell, and give their blessing to the soul of Donn. But as for the righteous soul of a penitent, it beholds the place from afar and is not borne astray. Such, at least, is the belief of the heathen. Hence Tech Duinn is so called.

ABOVE: **Míl Espaine, Breogan's son, is a shadowy figure even by mythic standards: his name means, simply, "Spanish Soldier".**

THE WARS OF ULSTER

2

What the War of Troy was to the classical world, the Wars of Ulster became to Irish Celtic culture – a mythic conflict in which a heroic identity had been forged.

The *Sídhe*, we saw, lived inside earthen mounds, and there have been those who said that Emain Macha, outside Armagh, was one such dwelling-place, but modern archeologists have found no trace of the fairy people. Neither have they excavated any evidence of the existence of the ancient war goddess Macha, nor of the race she reportedly ran (and won) against the chariot of Ulster's king. Still less can they confirm the tradition that, at the race's finishing line – right on this very spot – the goddess collapsed not only in exhaustion but in labour in the moment of her triumph. There and then, screaming fit to bring down the heavens in her pain, she gave birth to a pair of baby boys. (The old Irish name *Emain Macha* means, literally, the "Twins of Macha".) In her agony, the stories say, she called down a curse

OPPOSITE: **Cú Chulainn,** bewitched into weakness, tied himself to a standing stone to die on his feet, dispatched by a traitor's poisoned sword.

upon the men of Ulster: from that time on, for nine generations, whenever their kingdom was threatened with war – just when they needed to be at their peak pitch of readiness to come to its defence – they would find themselves immobilized, racked by pangs to match those of childbirth. These cramps were to continue for five full days. This imprecation delivered, the goddess promptly died.

Despite the *dindshenchas'* testimony, the excavators' findings seemed (at least at first) to confirm the more down-to-earth conclusion that this place must have been quite simply a military stronghold, its prominent mound – 40m (130ft) high and 250m (820ft) across – defensive in its purpose. Hence its modern name "Fort Navan", "Navan" being the nearest the Anglo-Saxon tongue could come to reproducing the sound of the original Gaelic *An Emain*.

More recently, however, researchers have wondered why – if this were really just the workaday hillfort it appears to be at first glance – its "defensive" ditches and ramparts lay within the stone- and timber-built structures they were seemingly protecting. Increasingly, the tendency has been to assume – although there's never really any certainty in such matters – that "Fort Navan" was actually a ceremonial centre of some kind. While we are, accordingly, quite some way short of a scientific confirmation of the goddess's story, this does suggest that Emain Macha may not have had a straightforward defensive role. At least to some extent, it seems to have been a religious monument, a place of ritual – and, like the fairy mound it was so long taken for, a structure with connections to two very different worlds. One, a world of religious mystery, of gods and spirits; the other

BELOW: **Hardly a home for heroes, Fort Navan today reminds us how remote these mythical times have become in Ireland's past.**

of temporal power, of practical politics – and, yes, inevitably, of military defence and conquest. For, with as vivid a presence in Irish myth as on the Armagh ground, Fort Navan/Emain Macha may be seen today as uniting those two realms.

ABOVE: **Viewed from above, Emain Macha makes a more impressive sight, though it isn't easily imaginable as a seat of kings.**

A Human History

It was here, according to the legend, that the *Ulaid* had their capital, and it was within these fortifications that their kings made their home. The people who were one day destined to give their name to Ulster do appear to have existed, although their lives and history have become the stuff of myth. In the early centuries of the first millennium AD, their kingdom seems to have stretched across the whole of what is now the British province of Northern Ireland, although it extended down into Co. Louth in the modern-day Republic. So remote is this period in history that it almost might as well be myth – especially given that it comes down to us in the form of poetic epics that were recorded

long afterwards by medieval monks. Unburdened by any modern sense of scholarly rigour, they were also untroubled by any feeling that the integrity of pagan narratives should be respected: on the plus side, they knew a gripping story when they heard it.

Their account of this epoch differs from their narrative of the *Tuatha Dé Danann*, however. Those stories described the deeds, experiences and feelings of a race of individuals who – despite their all-too-human frailties – were deities. In the stories of the Ulster Cycle, while the warriors often have superhuman powers and practised all sorts of witchcraft and enchantment, the characters are men and women rather than gods, and events are acted out on a much more human scale. Some scholars have suspected that, in their original state in the pagan oral tradition, these stories concerned a cast of gods and goddesses, and that their enactment here by human mortals represents a conscious "demotion" on the Christian chroniclers' part. If this is so (and how can we know for sure?), it has at least the advantage of making the characters live and resonate more humanly, and so more vividly in the modern mind. The wars between the *Ulaid* and their enemies – most notably the Connachta – may be touched by magic and tilted by the rivalries of godlike heroes, but they're driven by emotions that all us mortals can comprehend.

OPPOSITE: **The ancient bard or storyteller traditionally accompanied himself with music on his harp.**

A Controversy Conceived

It was in the reign of Eochaid Sálbuide (Eochaid Yellowheel) that, the storytellers say, the quarrel started. It began with the conception of Conchobar. One day, the king's daughter, Princess Ness, was sitting outside the royal residence at Emain Macha with her attendants when she saw Cathbad, the court's chief druid, walking by. "What", she asked him, "is this a good day

ULSTER-ON-SEA

From the fifth century, in strictly historical terms, the *Ulaid* started to be pushed back by their aggressive rivals into their territories to the east of the River Bann. By this time, though, they had started opening up colonies across the North Channel in Scotland's southwestern Highlands and Islands (the very name Argyll means "eastern country of the Gael"). This became the basis for the strong and successful kingdom of Dál Riata, which straddled both these coasts. In a time when land travel was difficult at best, especially across rugged terrain, it made perfect sense to have a stretch of sea as a sort of central plaza that – rather than dividing the Irish and Scottish coasts – brought them together. The kingdom was named for its people's mythic progenitor, Eochu Riata. This founder's

"footprint" may still be seen (with a little imaginative effort) in a stone slab at Dunadd hillfort in Argyll (*see photograph right*), in later centuries the kingdom's capital. Although eaten away by Irish rivals in Ulster – and, in Scotland, beleaguered by the Picts to the north and east (and, eventually, by Viking raiders from the west) – Dál Riata was not finally to fall until the ninth century. All this while, of course, the *Ulaid* lived on in legend ….

for?" He answered promptly: "For a king to be conceived within a queen". Ness was not the woman to doubt or dither: she seized the moment – and the only man present, Cathbad himself. Bundling the bewildered priest inside, she took him to her quarters and pulled him down beside her and had sexual relations with him. By the time he left, the princess had conceived.

It was a long pregnancy: not until three years and three months later did she bear her baby son. She gave him the name of Conchobar. Conchobar mac Nessa ("Connor, Son of Ness") was generally acknowledged as the son of Cathbad, and the druid played his part in the boy's upbringing. Conchobar's life changed for ever at the age of seven, his mother having caught the eye of the new king, Fergus mac Róich, who asked Ness if she would become his queen. On one condition only, she said: she wanted her son to be able to claim that *his* son was the scion of a king, so she asked that Conchobar should be given Ulster's kingship for just a year. Fergus agreed, reassured by his advisors that no one would ever take a little boy's authority seriously. So Ness became his wife and queen and, for just a while, her son was anointed "king" – although no one was in any doubt where the real royal power lay.

Ness was not done yet, though. In the days and weeks that followed, she took all the livestock and possessions she had herself or could call up from her kinsfolk and handed them out among the warriors of Fergus on Conchobar's behalf. Already dismayed and disillusioned at the way the lord they'd served so loyally had seemingly bought and sold them in his matrimonial agreement, they were delighted at the generosity of the new king. So much so that, when the year was up and Fergus announced that he was going to resume his reign, his lords unanimously mutinied: they wanted Conchobar to continue on the throne. In the face of what amounted to a coup, Fergus mac Róich was forced to give up his claim to the kingship. Conchobar mac Nessa was officially affirmed as Ulster's king.

BELOW: Technology had underwritten the expansion of the Celts: these knives make a (strikingly literal) emblem of Iron Age progress.

OF MYTHS AND MEN

Between Fort Navan and the border stretches some of modern Ireland's loveliest countryside: green fields, drystone walls, small woods, moorland patches and sparkling streams. But, a couple of decades after the 1993 Downing Street Declaration ushered in the end of the Northern Irish "Troubles" (*see photograph above*), South Armagh's grim reputation as "Bandit Country" is still remembered. For across the fields and farms over which – in the legendary past – the Sons of Uisliu attacked Conchobar's kingdom, IRA snipers and British soldiers played cat-and-mouse. If Ulster is British, even now, that is a result of its historic rebelliousness, its insistent Irishness in the face of Anglo-Saxon rule. The "Plantation of Ulster" – the deliberate establishment of Scottish and English Protestant settlers in the seventeenth century – was a direct response to the refusal of local Gaelic (and Catholic) chieftains to toe the line. How far the combatants on either side in the 1970s or 80s could be said to be representing the finest traditions of their respective national traditions must be debatable. It is still striking, though, the way that myths persist, and the way they've slowly modulated over historic time in a part of Ireland which has, indeed, felt at best uncomfortable under British rule. Also, it is the way in which new myths are made – not least the label of "Bandit Country", applied by the British press, to a region whose inhabitants have for the most part wanted nothing more than peace.

A Great King

Conchobar grew into the role and, by the time he'd reached manhood, he was universally admired – even revered. So much so that the young men of Ulster were happy for him to take their brides to his own bed on their wedding nights – a true father to his people, in other words. Although as famous for his courage as for his wisdom, he was painstakingly protected by his warriors, who went before him into battle lest he should come to harm. For, if Cathbad's prophecy had been borne out, and Ness's son was every inch a king, the queen's desire that her son's son should be a king was yet to be.

Conchobar had three imposing houses: his personal residence was called Craebruad ("The Red Branch", red for his royalty); in Craebdearg ("Bright Red Branch") he kept his collection of severed heads, along with other trophies taken from his foes. The Téte Brec, or "Glittering Treasure", glittered indeed with jewelled chalices and plates, plus the gold and silver of decorated daggers, swords, spears and richly woven banners. Téte Brec was also home to spectacularly ornate shields, including the King's own, which he referred to as Ochain or "The Ear of Beauty".

ABOVE HIS HEAD HUNG A SILVER ROD WITH THREE GOLDEN APPLES.

Craebruad was absolutely vast, panelled throughout with yew for protection against harmful spells and spirits; in its 150 chambers dwelt almost 500 of Conchobar's warriors and their wives. He himself lived in the very heart of the house, and here too was the throne room in which he sat to receive his visitors and to issue orders. Above his head hung a silver rod tipped with three golden apples, at once a talisman and an emblem of the king's authority: the apples shook as a signal for silence when he wished to speak. Around the walls were rich, red copper screens across which exquisitely crafted birds of gold and silver appeared to flutter, the torchlight twinkling off the jewels that formed their eyes. An incomparably generous host, Conchobar kept a wondrous cauldron: Ol Nguala, or the "Coal Vat", so called for the deep black beer with which it was always brimming over. Having brought it back as booty from one of his raids, the king had placed it in his throne room so his heroes could come and drink their fill at any time.

RIGHT: Cast in bronze, a human figure, holding his arms outspread, makes a witty handle for a Celtic sword.

A Warning of War

Among Conchobar's closest comrades was his storyteller, Fedlimid mac Daill. One night Fedlimid called his king and all his fellow-warriors to a gathering in his quarters. While they drank and laughed and sang, his wife bustled about bringing fresh supplies, awkward in her movements because she was pregnant and near her time. Eventually, as it grew late, she felt tired: it was time for her to slip away discreetly, she decided, and take to her bed while the menfolk continued with their revelry. Such was the uproar that no one noticed as she quietly headed for the

LEFT: This "bucket" – wooden but wrapped in bronze – was found at Aylesford, Kent. It contained the cremated remains of human bones.

door – until, all of a sudden, the infant in her belly shrieked out an ear-splitting scream. Abruptly, the room fell silent: the men sat stunned, their gestures frozen, their looks alarmed. What horrendous sound, they wondered, had that been? Who could possibly have cried out with such terrible feeling? Fedlimid's wife simply stood there, transfixed with fear.

The company gazed at her, terrified. As some semblance of calm returned, her husband called her back to the centre of the room and asked if she had suffered some agonizing fit or spasm. She was unable to say: instead, stammering in her confusion, she begged the Druid Cathbad to explain to her how or why her womb could possibly have issued this appalling cry of anguish. It wasn't an infant who'd yelled out so shockingly, said Cathbad, but an adult and alluring woman with tumbling tresses of golden hair, twisting down beside the temples of her stunning face. Her eyes flashing green; her smile glinting white; her lips bright red; her cheeks gently flushed with the pink of foxglove flowers, she would enchant everyone who saw her with her dazzling looks,

BELOW: This Celtic chieftain's roundhouse was re-created on its original foundation at Castell Henllys, outside Newport in South Wales.

and heroes would do battle and wars would be fought on her account. "Deirdre, she will be named", he said, "and beautiful as she may be, she will bring with her only conflict and contention."

Not long after the baby girl was born, and once again Cathbad was called to prophesy. Addressing Deirdre herself this time, he gave this warning: "Your face and figure will make men weep, and women curl up inside with envy and resentment; your presence will set all Ulster at odds, daughter of Fedlimid. Your face, a flame of beauty, will fire fury throughout the kingdom: heroes will have to go into exile for its sake." He concluded with a promise: "You'll live for ever in your loveliness – but yours is not going to be a happy story. Rather, it will be a tale of wounds, death and bloodshed, and crimes of every kind, and its ending will be a grave in which you lie alone."

YOUR FACE, A FLAME OF BEAUTY, WILL FIRE FURY.

At this, a clamour arose: many of those present called for the child to be slaughtered on the spot. How could such a source of danger be allowed to live? But Conchobar overruled them. The girl should be taken away and brought up on his behalf. For the king had decided to keep her for himself. And so it was done: Deirdre grew to girlhood far from Conchobar's court in almost complete seclusion, her only human contact her foster-parents and her nurse Leborcham.

"Imagine a Man…"

One winter's day as, outside her home, her foster-father flayed a calf, young Deirdre saw a raven swoop down and start to peck at the bloodstained snow. It stirred a thought in her mind she admitted to Leborcham when she came out and joined her. Rather than reading in the raven a sign that things in her life might not end well, the optimistic maiden had seen the bird as an exciting omen. "Imagine a man with those three colours", she mused, "his hair as black as that raven's feathers, his cheeks red as blood and his skin as white as snow!" She would, she insisted, be ill until she met him.

Such a man did exist, her nurse told her, and he was in fact quite close at hand: his name was Naoise and he was the son

of Uisliu, Conchobar's younger brother. Eager to see this young paragon, Deirdre walked out one day as far as Emain: Naoise was standing on the ramparts, singing softly to himself, as she passed by. Thrilled at the sight of her beauty, he looked at her in wonderment but could have no doubt of who this stranger was. This was his uncle's intended, he knew: it was more than his life was worth to get involved with her. But he couldn't help letting slip a single compliment. "That's a handsome heifer", he said – to which the girl herself retorted: "What do you expect? The heifers grow well where there are no bulls to bother them." Naoise responded in kind: "You have the biggest bull in Ulster at your disposal. Aren't you the chosen lover of our great King Conchobar?"

"I'd rather have a younger animal," the girl replied, "are you saying that you're refusing me?" "I am indeed", said Naoise: "You are the king's." But Deirdre wasn't to be turned down: there and then, she seized the man she chose, grabbing him by the ears and pulling him to her, making him cry out in his astonishment and pain. Hearing a disturbance, Naoise's brothers came rushing out to assist him. Seeing their brother smitten, they were worried both on his behalf and Ulster's. Still, they could never conceive of deserting him: they agreed on the spot that they would leave with all their supporters and spirit the lovers away to safety.

On the Run

So they set off, and spent the months and years that followed on the move, flitting from place to place across the whole of Ireland, constantly harassed by the warbands Conchobar had sent in their pursuit. In time their travels took them across the sea to southwestern Scotland. There they lived beyond civilization, in the empty wastes and beyond the law, as brigands and cattle-raiders, taking what they could from outlying settlements as they went. Inevitably, their activities brought them into conflict with the King of Alba, to whose realm this corner of Scotland then belonged. To avoid a hopeless – and pointless – fight to the death, the Sons of Uisliu made an accommodation with the Scottish ruler, enlisting in his service as mercenaries.

All went well – the Ulstermen seemed finally to have found themselves a sanctuary, and they built themselves a little village, thinking now of staying and settling down. Even now, though, they proceeded with some caution, clustering their huts around the home of Naoise and Deirdre so that their princess should as far as possible be kept from view.

Their wariness proved well-founded but inadequate, unfortunately, for it wasn't long before the lovely Deirdre was observed. When word reached the King of Alba of the Irishwoman's

THEY LIVED BEYOND CIVILIZATION, IN THE EMPTY WASTES.

surpassing beauty, he started sending his messengers to pester her. Every day they went to wait on her, promising every imaginable inducement to come and see their king and sleep with him. Every evening they returned with her refusal.

Over time, the king's disappointment turned to anger. No longer welcome allies, the Sons of Uisliu were once more seen as interlopers and Alba's warriors began attacking them again. The hostilities growing in bitterness, the Ulstermen's position became increasingly untenable: they fought bravely, but their spirited

TRAPPED BY TABOO

It's hard for us now to appreciate the outrage early audiences must have felt on hearing of Conchobar's actions against Fergus mac Róich in this affair. Fergus is forced by the need to observe one iron law of Celtic custom – that of friendly acceptance of a comrade's hospitality – to break another: that of selling out a friend. The king's cold cynicism in hatching this plan is shocking: by deploying Fergus' own scrupulousness against him, he's not just ignoring but pretty much mocking social rules. Some scholars see Conchobar as a sort of Celtic Machiavelli. His actions generally, it is suggested, seem to represent the beginnings of a new and ruthlessly practical politics geared completely to opportunistic, earthly ends.

resistance only further infuriated the King of Alba. They were more or less marooned in enemy territory, far from home.

An Unhappy Homecoming

At last, the King called all his men together from across the entire length and breadth of Alba: he was going to take what he wanted, come what may. He knew that the Sons of Uisliu would fight to the death for Deirdre, but no matter, he would kill them all – nothing would stop him from having the Irish beauty for his queen. Hearing rumours of what was afoot, Deirdre called Naoise and his men together: she couldn't let them all be killed on her behalf. Somehow or other, they had to get away.

And so once again they fled for their lives, landing up this time on an offshore island – no more than a temporary refuge, that was clear. In the meantime, though, the news of Naoise's troubles had reached Ulster – Conchobar, of course, was not wholly displeased. With appropriate shows of reluctance, he let himself be talked into taking pity on their plight, eventually agreeing to the refugees' return. He made Fergus mac Róich – his former king and rival – his emissary, bearing a message to the Sons of Uisliu promising safe conduct

THE SONS OF UISLIU WOULD FIGHT TO THE DEATH FOR DEIRDRE.

to them if they came in peace. On his way home with them to Emain Macha, however, Fergus was waylaid by another courier from Conchobar, bidding him make a detour to attend a royal feast. Fergus couldn't with propriety reject such an invitation, so he was forced to leave his guests to continue on their way without him. The former king had served his purpose to the present one now: Fergus' departure left the Sons of Uisliu in a truly perilous position, the guarantee of their safe conduct now gone.

They were exposed as well to further prying: Conchobar, nothing if not calculating, wanted to be sure the treasure he was after had not lost "value" over time. He sent Deirdre's old nurse Leborcham out to meet the new arrivals and inspect the merchandise – just to be sure that all this contrivance was worthwhile. Leborcham's loyalties were to her old charge: deep down, she wanted her to be happy. She came back to the King with the news that Deirdre's charms had been fading fast. However, Conchobar was much too cunning to take her word alone: once the visitors had arrived at Emain Macha and been installed as guests in the Craebruad, a male messenger was sent to see, and returned with very different news. Deirdre, he reported, impossible as it might be to imagine, was still more beautiful than she'd been before.

Determined now to press ahead with his plan, Conchobar sent a deputation to the Red House to welcome the returners officially.

ABOVE: **Deirdre, defined by her sorrows now, delivers her heartfelt elegy for the dead Naoise.**

It was led by Eogan mac Durthact, a minor king who, having fallen out with Conchobar some time before, hoped by helping him now to win his way back to favour. As he spoke to Naoise, addressing him with all apparent respect and honour, he suddenly took his spear and ran him through. Before his startled supporters could react, battle had been joined: Conchobar's minions had snatched the initiative – and the wretched Deirdre. Although Naoise's brothers all fought bravely, they were finally forced to retreat and recoup their strength without her.

ABOVE: **Clutching Naoise's severed head, Deirdre sits and rocks, beyond all help and comfort in a wilderness of grief.**

Exiled anew, they left their native country: this time, though, their travels took them overland westward, across to Connacht, where King Ailill mac Máta and his Queen Medb (or Maeve) held sway. Bitter experience had left them without illusions: they knew well that the generous reception they had from the Connachta was based not on warmth towards them but on enmity to Ulster. But beggars could not be choosers – and, besides, it suited them to have the backing of Ailill in the war they were going to wage themselves with Conchobar. By now 3000 strong, they represented a formidable force, a little Ulster in exile, living autonomously but under the protection of Connacht's king. In the years that followed, they harried their homeland constantly, mounting repeated raids into Ulster's borderlands, slaying her sons and driving off her cattle. Fergus mac Róich fought alongside the exiles, furious that his old usurper had taken advantage of his good name and his good faith to work his wiles. Together they made every day a day of tragedy and mourning for Ulster's families, and Conchobar's life a misery.

Deirdre of the Sorrows

Not, however, quite as miserable as that of his reluctant companion Deirdre, who let an entire year go by without once so much as smiling, we are told. The king sent special gifts and treats of food and drink to coax her into compliance, as well as musicians to serenade her into cheerfulness, but nothing, it quickly became clear, could win her round. How was wine to woo a woman who had sat down to drink with the delightful Naoise?, she asked her waiters. What delicacies could compensate her for the diet of deep love she'd lost? Their airs and reels might entertain the king, she told his musicians, but she had known the lilting music of Naoise's voice, enjoyed the gentle harmony of her life with him.

"I have loved his golden hair," she said, "and his manly stature – standing tall as a tree. No point in my looking out for his fine form now, though, nor awaiting his homecoming. I loved his

"I LOVED HIM IN THE DAWN LIGHT, AS HE ROSE IN THE MORNING, WHERE WE CAMPED IN THE WOODS."

modest diffidence as much as I did his heroic strength; his gentle decorum as much as I did his burning desire; I loved him in the dawn light, as he rose in the morning, where we camped in the woods. Those blue eyes which made men tremble and women reel with yearning – I loved those too, of course, just as I did the reassuring sound of his singing voice as we made our way through the forest's darkest depths. Without him, I lie sleepless at night and get up only to dawdle through my days: I see no reason to

BELOW: Seen here by Scottish artist John Duncan (1866–1945), Deirdre became emblematic of a certain "Celtic" sensibility of suffering.

paint my nails or make myself look beautiful, to smile or even eat. What pleasure can I take in company? In the pomp and ceremony of the court? In the crowds of nobles here? What palace could be grand enough to distract me from my grief?"

Transported by a beauty that was now only enhanced by her air of melancholy, King Conchobar fell for Deirdre deeply and genuinely. As the days and weeks went by, however, and his beloved showed no sign of softening, his love started giving way to rancour. Deirdre didn't care, nor did she fear the king, however high his anger: she wasn't long for this life anyway, she told him. He tried to punish her, asking her what in the world she most hated:

after Conchobar himself, she said, her lover's killer, Eogan mac Durthact. Then, the king said cruelly, he would send her to stay with Eogan: she could look forward to living with Naoise's murderer night and day. The next morning, Eogan mac Durthact was sent for: he left with Deirdre beside him in his chariot. How lucky she was, crowed Conchobar – between him and Eogan, Deirdre was like a lustful ewe with two fine rams to choose from.

Finally provoked from her passivity by that spiteful sneer, she flung herself from the chariot, dashing her head against a rock, and died there and then.

Cú Chulainn Conceived

Conchobar's reign continued, but his kingdom still seemed to be accursed. One day, a flock of birds descended on Ulster's fields in what appeared a feeding frenzy. Stripping the country bare before them, they advanced across the realm. Conchobar called his men together to join him in a bird hunt. Conchobar's sister, Deichtine, decided to go along with her brother and her husband, Sualtam mac Róich, and off they all went in hot pursuit, riding in their chariots as though to a war with men. But these were magical birds, and they could not seem to reach them. Crossing the sky in pairs, each yoked to its mate by a silver chain, the marauding raiders were formed into larger groups – a score in each; wondering villagers counted nine such squadrons flying over.

Heading south, the king and his company soon found themselves approaching the valley of the Boyne in what we now call Co. Meath. Caught out by a blizzard, they decided to stop

Irish Emblem

There are Irish myths, and then there's Deirdre. Her story has just about everything, from intoxicating beauty through betrayal to star-crossed love and tragic death. More to the point, perhaps, the legendary heroine embodies all those qualities held to be quintessentially "Celtic" in the modern view, while in her destiny that of Ireland may be seen. At the time of the early twentieth-century "Celtic Twilight", indeed, no fewer than five plays were produced with Deirdre's story at the centre. Her life inspired such luminaries as W.B. Yeats, J.M. Synge and George Russell (or "AE").

Key to her appeal was the deep-running ambiguity that allowed her to be "read' simultaneously as sexual temptress and as damsel in distress; to represent a femininity that could be both sinister and sentimentalized. On the one hand an Irish Helen of Troy, her beauty brought great heroes into conflict – and, ultimately, to a dreadful death; on the other, she was an innocent victim, betrayed and abused. For Synge, it seems, it was the sheer sadness of Deirdre's story that appealed; Yeats's view (surprisingly, in such a mystic) was worldlier. A strand of political allegory in his play establishes Conchobar as the embodiment of a boorish and bullying imperial power – not wholly unlike that of England over the Irish, in his view.

where they were for the night. Seeking shelter, they could only find a little cottage in which a couple were living. Poor as they were, they opened up their home to their distinguished guests.

In the night, though, the noise of a disturbance was heard. The man of the house appeared, explaining that his wife, who had been with child, was giving birth. Deichtine, the only other woman present, went to her assistance and successfully delivered a baby boy. Meanwhile, a mare in the stable was delivered of twin foals. Next morning, when they all awoke, the cottage and the couple who had lived there – and the birds – were gone. Looking about them, all they could see was open country: they were, it has traditionally been believed, on the main mound of the complex known as Brú na Bóinne (one of Ireland's most impressive megalithic monuments, this neolithic burial site, in a bend of the River Boyne, is often also referred to as Newgrange). But the boy was there, as were the newborn foals. Interpreting this as an omen, the royal company decided Deichtine should adopt the infant and take the foals along with them as a gift for him. Deichtine cared for the growing boy as if he were her own and she was utterly distraught when, not long after, he took sick and died. Sobbing herself hoarse, and brought to a raging thirst, she asked for wine – but when she drank it a tiny homunculus slipped from the cup into her mouth and down into her insides. There it grew till it was her turn to give birth to a handsome baby boy, whom she named Sétanta. (A handsome and remarkable boy, it may have been the ambiguities around his parentage and his strange manner of conception that freed him from the infirmity inflicted on his countrymen by Macha's curse. Deichtine's labour pangs appear to have done for him as well: when trouble threatened and, as the goddess had warned, Ulster's warriors writhed helplessly around, incapable of action, he would be hale and fit and ready for action.)

CULANN UNLEASHED THE GIANT HOUND HE KEPT TO GUARD HIS HOME.

Sétanta, Son of Ulster

Since no one knew who his father was – or if he even really *had* one – Conchobar's warriors vied with one another for the honour of rearing Sétanta. Finally a druid decreed that he should be brought up by the king himself. His warriors should contribute to his upbringing, each inculcating in the boy his own particular talents, skills and qualities so he'd grow up rounded and finished, a paragon in every way. Amergin mac Eccit, a famous poet, was given a special responsibility as his tutor, while his wife Finnchaem was to be his foster-mother.

Under their guidance, Sétanta grew up firm in his physique, true and brave in his temperament, formidable in arms but gentle and courteous in his manner and eloquent – even poetic – in his speech. He'd shown his courage and composure early on: even at the age of five or six, he'd been a star in the sporting field, his exploits in one hurling match – just him against 150 much older boys – such that an admiring Conchobar, watching, had invited him to join him that evening at a feast he would be attending. It was to be held at the home of the smith Culann, but Conchobar forgot to tell him about his extra guest, so once the King had arrived, Culann unleashed the giant hound he kept to guard his home. Three chains were needed to hold him, and three men had to hold each chain for this ferocious animal to be kept in line.

Now, though, this monstrous dog was running free through the enclosed area around Culann's home. The little boy, strolling up a while later, seemed utterly defenceless as the beast sprang for his throat. With a wave of his stick, however, he hit a hurley ball down the dog's throat and killed it, and Sétanta simply continued on his way. So upset was the smith to lose his hound that the young Sétanta promised to train him up a new one: while this one was growing, he would keep watch over the house himself, willingly serving as Culann's Hound and taking the name *Cú Chulainn*.

LEFT: Sétanta slays the hound of Culann: the exploit that would end up giving him his nom de guerre, Cú Chulainn.

The Wooing of Emer

Approaching manhood, Cú Chulainn was unsurpassable in his looks: to the women who saw him he seemed irresistible. So much so that Conchobar's warriors grew alarmed. A wife was going to have to be found for this handsome young man, it was agreed, so Ulster's husbands could have some peace of mind! Emissaries were sent out the length and breadth of Ireland to find a maiden beautiful enough to marry this young paragon, but Cú Chulainn already knew who he wanted for his bride. Her name was Emer, and she was the daughter of Forgall Monach. Setting out to woo her in his chariot, he met her on the road as she

BELOW: **Cú Chulainn chose Emer over all Ireland's other beauties.**

walked with her girlfriends: she fell in love with him at first sight, and all over again when she heard him speak.

Emer's father was less amenable, though. Reluctant to let him have his daughter, Forgall set the young man a challenge: he had to go to Alba to train in arms under the Scáthach, or the "Woman of Shadows". This Celtic Amazon – a renowned warrior – was said to have dwelt in Dun Sgathaich (Dunscaith), later to be a famous seat of the Clan MacDonald but at this time just another hillfort on the coast of Skye.

Forgall's intention, clearly, was that the young man would not return from what promised to be a perilous mission: the Scáthach's students often died before they could complete her course. But Cú Chulainn cheerfully accepted his challenge: journeying to Skye, he enlisted in the Scáthach's school and quickly won her respect, lasting loyalty and trust. Fighting alongside his teacher, he helped her to victory over her sister – and her most bitter rival – Aoife. Having challenged him to single combat, this warrior woman shattered Cú Chulainn's sword at a single blow, but he was able to overcome her none the less. In return for her life, Aoife agreed to bear him a son and bring him up till he reached the age of seven, when she'd send him to Ireland to find his father. She slept with the hero who, before he left, gave her his ring for his future son to wear: that way, when he found him, he would know him. The young boy would be called Connla, but was on no account to reveal his name to anyone.

Already a fine warrior when he first set foot in Skye, Cú Chulainn returned to his native Ireland the greatest hero Europe had ever seen. He found, however, that Forgall had taken advantage of his absence to offer Emer's hand to King Lugaid mac Nóich of Munster. The latter, by no means unwilling, had got as far as coming to Forgall's fortress home to collect his bride – but on learning of Cú Chulainn's interest, he had withdrawn his own. Coming back to claim his bride, Cú Chulainn was to have a long and bitter fight of it: it took him a year to battle his way through the armies Forgall had placed around his home. The way once clear, however, he brought up his chariot and charged the last line of defence, killing over 300 men and bursting into the hall where Forgall was. Scything right and left with his sword, he spared only Emer's brothers among the menfolk present: Forgall himself took flight, but fell from his own battlements to his death. Seeing Emer standing trembling with her beloved foster-sister and companion by her side, Cú Chulainn scooped both up in his arms and they escaped.

ABOVE: **Queen Medb walks out to meet the young Cú Chulainn: the start of what was to be a fateful feud.**

ABOVE: Cú Chulainn as seen by Scottish painter Stephen Reid, from his classic illustrations to Eleanor Hull's *The Boys' Cuchulain* (1904).

A Matter of Honour

We tend to think of myths and legends as representing the values of the ancient past in the modern present: by definition, they show aspects of the world that have since changed. Sometimes, though, they illustrate the limitations of tradition and the downright necessity of reforming old attitudes. One such example is the story of Cú Chulainn's triumphant return to Emain Macha with his beautiful bride. Only when they made their entrance was it recalled that Emer would – by established custom – have to sleep with Conchobar. If it was out of the question that so great a hero as Cú Chulainn should have to share his wife, it was out of the question too that Conchobar shouldn't have his "first night" privilege. In the end, a compromise was reached: while Emer would spend the night in the king's bed, so too would two of Conchobar's most senior officials – his druid father Cathbad and his royal predecessor, Fergus mac Róich – to make sure that nothing untoward took place.

Parallel Lives

To us, perhaps, these ancient Irish legends conjure up a profoundly alien time, however heroic it may be. Warriors live by an honour code that has little in common with our present-day morality; the omens that move them (whether to fear or rejoicing) owe nothing either to modern religion or to science. Even so, we have to bear in mind that these stories have been transmitted to us by monkish scribes: if we owe them thanks for that, some scepticism is appropriate as well. For the most part, perhaps, we can only speculate on the sorts of changes they made (many scholars believe that the Ulster Cycle's heroes were deities in earlier versions, for example).

LEFT: "The Annunciation", a painting by Luca Giordano. Much is made in Celtic myth that Conchobar's birth coincided with that of Christ, rooting the story firmly in Christian chronology.

At times, though, they show their hand – and their arguable conflict of interest – only too clearly: much is made in the extant texts, for instance, of the fact that Conchobar's birth coincided exactly with that of Christ. This may seem strange, given the less-than-edifying example this early king of Ulster would appear to set, but it does have the effect of anchoring the Irish story in a Christian chronology.

Cú Chulainn also has his Christ-like aspects, and nowhere more strikingly than in his conception: a parallel the mythic account seems almost to go out of its way to draw. Deichtine is a married woman at the start of the story, and there's no suggestion that her marriage to Sualtam mac Róich has gone unconsummated, but her son's conception is very obviously non-sexual. In some versions of the legend, indeed, we're told that, before bearing Sétanta, Deichtine is "made whole and virgin" – as though she's to be a Celtic Mary and Cú Chulainn another Christ.

BELOW: Once the central chamber of a burial mound, Proleek Dolmen, outside Dundalk, now stands as a memorial to ancient mysteries.

A Tragic Reunion

Their wedding festivities over, Cú Chulainn and Emer set up home in the hero's stronghold in Dún Dealgán (or Dundalk). They were as happy together as any couple could be. Meanwhile, however, back in Skye Cú Chulainn's son Connla was growing. At the age of seven, as agreed, Aoife sent the young boy off to Ireland to find his father. She had taught him all she knew about fighting – which of course was a great deal – so he was already a match for just about any warrior. He was accordingly unfazed when, as one day he walked up to Dún Dealgán, he found himself confronting Conall Cernach, one of Cú Chulainn's finest warriors. Challenged to reveal who he was, Connla refused to give his name, in keeping with the commitment his own father had exacted before his birth. Conall attacked him and was promptly and ignominiously disarmed. Cú Chulainn came out now to see what the commotion was all about. He too asked the boy to state his name, and again Connla refused – although he admitted that, had it not been for the prohibition he lived under he would have cheerfully complied, for he saw something in his challenger's face to which he could relate. Neither saw the significance of this, however, and so they fought.

At first it appeared that Cú Chulainn was also to be humiliated: the young boy whirled his sword about his body a time or two, then, in a single hissing stroke, shaved the hair clean off the hero's head. So small was he that he had to stand on a high rocky step – Tracht Esi, a beach in Co. Louth – in order to grapple with his opponent: some claim that the marks where his feet sank into the stone as he wrestled may still be seen. Into the sea itself they went, each one trying to duck and drown the other and failing until finally Cú Chulainn reached for the *Gáe Bolg*, a wicked thrusting spear with barbs, made from the bones of some fearful sea monster, which the Scáthach had given him and shown him

THE *GÁE BOLG* WAS A WICKED THRUSTING SPEAR WITH BARBS MADE FROM BONES.

BELOW: **Emer rebukes Cú Chulainn for his infidelity.**

AN INFIDELITY ERASED

Cú Chulainn had countless lovers: no woman could resist his handsomeness or his great strength; Emer was content enough to look the other way. Only one affair really rankled with her: her husband's love for Fand, fair wife of the Sea King, Manannán mac Lir, was of a different order. Fand had first appeared to him when flying in the form of a seabird with her sister Lí Ban. Cú Chulainn had thrown stones at these "birds" as they passed, infuriating them. Landing and taking on the form of spirit-women, they'd horsewhipped the hero so badly that he'd lain sick for a year, unable to move. Even then, he'd only been cured (or, rather, released from the spell that Fand had placed upon him) when he agreed to help her fight her enemies. They'd become lovers on the battlefield, and this was one relationship that Emer didn't see herself being able to compete with. Roused to a rage,

she came for Cú Chulainn with a band of her women friends, all wielding knives. Moved by the wronged wife's emotion and shamed by her sincerity, Fand decided to release her hold over her man. Her husband Manannán, relieved, waved his cloak of oblivion between his wife and Cú Chulainn – all was forgotten now, as though it had never been.

how to use. Never initiated in its use himself, young Connla was unable to resist. He lay helpless now as his lifeblood ebbed away. Only now, as Cú Chulainn stooped to look over his foe's fallen body did he see the thick ring his mother Aoife had made him wear – the ring that marked his slain enemy as his own son.

Pig-Headed

One of legendary Ireland's worst wars began with a bitter quarrel between two pig-keepers – although for years before they had been the best of friends. Friuch was in the service of Ochne, a local ruler in Connacht; Rucht worked for Bodb, whose kingdom was in Munster. No ordinary peasants, they were lauded far and wide for their way with the pigs they tended – but they were also famous for their skill in shape-shifting. Eventually, inevitably perhaps, they started to see each other as competitors; finally they fell out and tried to do one another down. At last, in the guise of hawks, they fought beak and claw for two years straight, followed by another two trying to devour each other in the shape of sea creatures. After that, they clashed as stags; then they were warriors and after that a pair of ghosts before they took the form of dragons and tangled furiously in one another's coils.

THEY FOUGHT BEAK AND CLAW FOR TWO YEARS STRAIGHT.

Finally they became maggots, in which form one fell into the River Cruind at Cuailnge (Cooley, in what is now Co. Louth, in the far south of ancient Ulster); the other into Connacht's River Garaid. The first was swallowed down unwittingly in a drink of water by a cow belonging to Dáire mac Fiachna, a local landowner; the second by a cow that was owned by King Ailill. Both cows conceived, the maggots growing and transforming into bull-calves within their wombs: they were reborn as bulls and grew up to be of an impressive size. Two mighty bulls, then, each in one of the north of Ireland's great rival kingdoms: one in Ulster and the other in Connacht. Ulster's was brown, as its Gaelic name, *Donn Cuailnge*, reflected; Connacht's was called *Finnenbach Ai*. This name referred to its most striking features, its snow-white face and feet, although its body was a deep and vibrant red.

A Marital Spat

One night as they lay in bed, Ailill and Medb were conversing happily when the king commented upon the queen's good fortune. How lucky she was, he mused contentedly, to have married so powerful and rich a ruler! How fate had smiled upon her, attaching her to so illustrious a lord. Proud Medb couldn't help but bridle: much as she loved her husband, she knew well that he'd been nothing but a bodyguard when she, herself the daughter of a king, had been married to Eochaid Dála, King of Connacht. (Before that she'd briefly been wed to Conchobar, but this unhappy union had left her with a lasting hostility to Ulster.) She had chosen Ailill as her husband because she admired his manly strength and courage more than she did Eochaid's royal status – but he couldn't seriously pull rank on her in this way!

All night they argued and the next day, far from giving up their quarrel, they continued it: now, by the light of day, they could compare their wealth, lining up their possessions in public view. Herds of cattle, horses and pigs and flocks of sheep were

ABOVE: Beyond the megalithic cemetery at Carrowmore, Knocknarea rears up against the Sligo horizon, the cairn of Queen Medb visible on top.

driven to the palace on their orders; mountains of jewellery and gold were heaped outside. When everything had been counted up and their respective worths had been calculated, the couple came out exactly matched in wealth.

Buying a Bull

Except in one thing: Ailill of course had the great white-headed bull, Finnenbach Ai. Rich as she was, Medb had nothing that could quite compare. Determined not to be outdone, she summoned Mac Roth, the royal steward: where could she find

BELOW: As represented by US illustrator J.C. Leyendecker in 1911, Queen Medb is half attitude and half allure.

a bull as big as her husband's? she asked him. In Ulster, he said, there was a dark brown bull every bit as fine as – or still better than – Finnenbach Ai. Dáire mac Fiachna had the good fortune to be its owner. Medb immediately resolved that she had to have this bull to better her husband's: Mac Roth must make his way to Ulster straight away, she said. In return for a year's loan of Donn Cuailnge, she'd give him 50 young heifers and a big parcel of the Plain of Ai – plus, perhaps, a richly accoutred chariot. And if it came to it, she was prepared to pay him with a "welcome from her thighs".

Off went Mac Roth's messengers: Dáire was ecstatic when he heard all the things that the Queen of Connacht was offering him – just for the year-long loan of his Donn Cuailnge – and agreed to her terms without hesitation. All seemed happy and harmonious until some of Dáire's attendants heard Mac Roth's men commenting that, if Dáire had not agreed, they would simply have come back with an army and taken the bull by force. Dáire wasn't too bothered by this remark, but the suggestion that their lord could not keep what was his without Connacht's say-so seemed to his henchmen to reflect badly on them. Offended, they went to confront Dáire, who now felt obliged to make some sort of stand and sent back word to Medb that his bull was not for her.

> DÁIRE WAS ECSTATIC WHEN HE HEARD WHAT THE QUEEN WAS OFFERING.

An Army Assembles

Connacht's queen was incandescent when the news reached her in the royal capital at Cruachan. Who did Dáire mac Fiachna think he was? Ailill too was outraged, his quarrel with Medb forgotten in his fury that a minor lord of Ulster should show such defiance to his wife. Now in full agreement, they determined

MEDB'S METROPOLIS?

Just off the N5 Longford–Westport Road, a little way north of Tulsk in Co. Roscommon, a large, flat-topped mound may be seen in the middle of a field. Closer up, this proves to be just one of a number of earthworks clustered around. Rathcroghan, as the place is now known, seems to have been an important religious and ceremonial centre, dating back several millennia before the events of the seventh-century epic, the *Táin Bó Cúailnge* ("Cattle Raid of Cooley"). Many scholars believe that Queen Medb was originally an earth goddess. There's no real evidence of a royal residence – or even any significant settlement – here, but it has traditionally been regarded as having been Connacht's ancient capital, Cruachan.

Untroubled by archeological scruples, the old storytellers went into considerable detail about a palace of pine with 16 windows, each framed with brass. The royal apartment, at the centre of the building, was walled with bronze and silver; the entire construction was covered over by a shingle roof.

What modern archeologists certainly *have* found evidence for is the use of this ancient complex as a cemetery – a sort of city of the dead. In fact, the folk tradition acknowledges this function too. Every summer at Samhain, it was long believed, the barrows or burial mounds at Rathcroghan would spontaneously open, unleashing a tide of ghosts, spirits and monsters upon the world. At their head would ride the Morrigan, her chariot pulled by a one-legged horse, spoiling for bloodshed, violence and rapine.

ABOVE: Medb as she appeared on the pre-Euro Punt Éreannach, with Celtic-style lettering in the background.

that they would do whatever it took to bring Donn Cuailnge back to their kingdom in the west. Sending out messengers to every corner of the realm, they called up all the men of fighting age in Connacht – and Ulster's exiled warriors, still living on their land. Now in fact the "Sons of Uisliu" were under the leadership of a son of Conchobar: Ulster's king had fathered Cormac Connlongas on his own mother, Ness. Never close to Conchobar, Cormac had been brought up by Fergus mac Róich and had followed his foster-father when he'd left Ulster years before. With their supporters, the Ulstermen were some 3000 strong.

Forebodings of Blood

"This army has been brought together in my name," Medb observed to her charioteer as they waited at the head of the line for the signal to move off. "On my orders, couples are being prised apart; lovers are leaving – perhaps never to be seen again. Many will be cursing me at this moment." As the charioteer turned his vehicle to catch the best of the sun's rays with their promise of a safe return, he and his mistress both caught sight of a beautiful young woman. Her flaxen hair falling gracefully on to shoulders draped by a mottled cloak, held in place by a glowing golden pin,

"THIS ARMY HAS BEEN BROUGHT TOGETHER IN MY NAME," MEDB OBSERVED.

she too was standing in a chariot. Intrigued by her beauty and her poise, Medb asked her name. "Fedelm", she replied. "I am a poet and a prophetess. I come from Connacht, but have been learning my trade in Alba." Pressing her to know if she had "second sight" and could offer insights into the future, the anxious queen asked how she saw the prospects for her army. "Blood-red", she retorted. "I see a war-host drenched in the red of blood, as though entirely cut down by Cú Chulainn, Ulster's hero." Medb refused to accept this prediction: Fedelm must be mistaken, she reasoned. Even now, she knew,

Conchobar's forces would be completely incapacitated, writhing around on the floor, racked with the labour pangs that Macha had condemned them to.

But Fedelm was firm in her insistence: three times Medb asked her how she saw her army; three times she answered flatly "blood-red". The fourth time she said the same thing too, but then she suddenly burst into a song of prophecy, describing the vision she was seeing of a tall, blond hero wreaking single-handed havoc among Medb's host. He looked, said Fedelm, for all the world like Ulster's celebrated champion, the great Cú Chulainn, and the might of Connacht was collapsing in his path. His comrades might be back in Ulster in the throes of imaginary labour, but Cú Chulainn was of course specifically exempted from the goddess' curse, and he alone could do the work of a whole army. Slashing about him with four swords in each hand, thrusting before him with a wicked-looking *Gáe Bolg* spear, he stood straight and calm in his chariot, his blood-red cloak trailing in the wind as he hurtled on. "I keep nothing hidden", Fedelm concluded. "Cú Chulainn leaves behind him a trail of mangled corpses and women's tears."

BELOW: In some versions a druid tries to warn Medb of the folly of her enterprise.

The Táin Trail

Surviving scripts of the *Táin Bó Cúailnge* ("Cattle Raid of Cooley") meticulously record the Connacht army's route across Ireland from Cruachan in Roscommon to Cooley, Co. Louth. They don't, however, do so consistently although it does seem that Medb and her men first set off to the southeast, passing Ardakill, Roscommon, at its site beside the lake. Heading on to Granard, the capital of what was then North Tethba in present-day Co. Longford, they then pushed eastward across the Irish Midlands towards the town of Kells, in what is now Co. Meath. Here they faced thick woodland, which they had to fell to make their way: hence the name *Slechta* ("Cut Road") by which this stretch of country, near the village of Kilskeer, was long known.

On they went, pressing quickly northeastward now: the ford at which Cú Chulainn held them up by planting a forked tree in their path was at what is now Kellystown, near Collon in Co. Louth. Their course then took them north through what is now Drogheda and beyond. Glen Gat, where the bull was briefly penned, is now a suburb of Dundalk. Sliab Cuilinn (now Slieve Gullion), where Donn Cuailnge then fled, rises southwest of Newry.

BELOW: The Normans raised this mound at Granard to build a castle, long after Queen Medb's army could have passed this way.

On the March

Medb was not to be diverted, though: off she went at the head of her host. It took some time for so vast an army to start moving. In addition to the Connachta and the Ulster exiles, she had called upon allies from Munster, far to the southwest, while there were 3000 Galeóin warriors from Leinster, in the east, as well. With so many men behind her it was difficult for the queen not to feel confident despite the warnings of Fedelm. That mood of optimism was general, and it lasted until the middle of the second day when the army's rest was rudely interrupted by the yelling of Dubthach Dóelthach, a friend of Fergus. He had also seen a vision, it seemed: he too saw a single warrior barring their way to Ulster backed by the deep waters of Cooley's River Cruind. Medb and Ailill now gave Fergus the lead: the route he chose took them arcing well to the south, and the royal couple wondered if was he trying to give old friends in Ulster time to organize. Approaching Iraird Cuillen – now Crossakiel, a few miles west

ABOVE: **Slieve Gullion rises high above the Armagh countryside: the Brown Bull of Cooley fled across these slopes.**

ABOVE: **Bronze could be beautifully worked, so still had ceremonial value well into the Iron Age. These swords were all found in Ireland.**

of Kells in Co. Meath – they put this concern to him, but he strenuously denied having any treacherous intent. Rather, he insisted, he was trying to find a way of outflanking Cú Chulainn, who he knew would be waiting somewhere along their way, ready to stop their vast army in its tracks.

Fork-Branch Ford

A heavy snowfall slowed them down, but even so they stole a march on Cú Chulainn, who had been drinking hard and overslept. By the time he woke, all he could see of his enemy were their tracks. This, however, was enough to enable him to estimate their number, pretty much exactly: 18 troops, each of 3000 men, had passed this way. Circling round and cutting across country, Cú Chulainn quickly outflanked and overtook the Connachtmen again. Four of their advance guard appeared and challenged him, but he quickly killed and beheaded them: he felled a forked tree with a single stroke of his sword and set their heads upon its branches. There, where the River Mattock was comparatively shallow, he hurled it like a javelin, and it

stuck, quivering, in the centre of the ford. Now no chariot could
pass this way: Cú Chulainn carved into its trunk a warning that
he had set this obstacle up himself without assistance; it could
only be removed by a man who could do it single-handed the
same way.

As Ailill and Medb and their leading warriors debated among
themselves who could have set up this sign, Fergus assured
them it couldn't have been anyone but Cú Chulainn. Medb was
unperturbed – by all accounts this mighty hero was still just a
stripling of 17 – but Fergus filled them in on the boyhood exploits
of Ulster's "Hound". No fighter could be more formidable, he
warned; no lion wilder; no hammer harder; no soldier could

WRONG WRITING?

Cú Chulainn's resort to writing when issuing his challenges
to Connacht's warriors is an anachronistic feature of the
surviving scripts of the *Táin Bó Cúailnge*. In their original
form, these stories would not of course have been written
down. As we've seen, the early Celts didn't use written script
– nor, despite having travelled, traded and settled the length
and breadth of Europe, did they make any use of the other
written languages available to them in their time. They're
assumed to have had some religious objection to doing so.
This didn't mean a lack of literature in its broadest sense –
they obviously had their own well-loved stories and poetry
– although of course, strictly speaking, literature has literally
to be written down. But many ancient epics appear to have
been handed down for generations through the oral tradition
before being finally recorded in written script: the *Iliad* and *Odyssey* of Homer, for example.

It seems certain, then, that Cú Chulainn's literacy is a Christian refinement to the original tales,
although it's interesting that, even so, the texts insist upon his using Ogham script, not the more
sophisticated Latin characters used later by Irish scribes. Rows of vertical lines with cross-strokes
for the most part carved into stone megaliths and suchlike (*see photograph above*), Ogham was a
comparatively rough and ready form of script. To the initiated, indeed, it seems like little more
than a row of notches. However, there's a pattern to the way the cross-strokes are clustered, while
the ways they angle to the vertical edge also appear to add meaning to those who know how to
read them. While the *Táin Bó Cúailnge* was written down in Roman script, these references to
Ogham were perhaps preferred for the suggestion they gave of a poem set in an earlier, less learned
but more manly and heroic time.

match his skill with weaponry. Still, reasoned Connacht's queen, he's a mortal man, and he only has one body. We can wound him in our thousands; he can't defeat us all. Fergus shook his head: in the end, after a succession of Connacht's finest had failed to pull the fork from the river bottom with a single tug, the exiled Ulsterman had to remove the obstacle himself. Even then, he had to make a great many attempts: no fewer than 14 chariots broke beneath him as he made repeated passes at the tree through the rushing water.

Another Obstacle

The forked branch finally removed, Ailill was able to give the signal to advance; the Connachtmen were on the march again. But another tree awaited them a little further along the road at a place called *Mag Muceda*, the "Pig Keepers' Plain". A sturdy oak, it lay full-square across their path and bore an Ogham inscription asserting that they should not pass until one of their number had jumped it in his chariot at the first attempt. Along with the 14

CÚ CHULAINN PRACTICALLY PLEADED WITH HIS ADVERSARY TO SEEK QUARTER.

Fergus had written off at the Forked-Branch Ford, 30 more were now destroyed, their horses killed and their charioteers badly shaken as the flower of Connacht's youth attempted in vain to clear the hurdle. The stretch was ever after known as *Belach nAne* ("The Place they Drove"). Finally, despairing, they sent Fraech mac Fidaig to challenge Cú Chulainn to a more conventional fight: he found him bathing at the place known ever after as *Ath Froich* ("Fraech's Ford"). It ended badly for Fraech, of course: having boasted that he'd overcome the youth with ease, he found himself quickly overpowered as they wrestled in the river, his head pushed beneath the surface of the stream by Cú Chulainn who practically pleaded with his adversary to ask for quarter. The Connachtman couldn't contemplate this, and in all honour Cú Chulainn finally felt he had no alternative but to hold him firmly down until he was drowned. When Fraech was carried ashore, they say, women dressed in green emerged from a nearby mound and carried the dead man back into the ground with

OPPOSITE: **His victory over Fraech was as much a tragedy as a triumph for Cú Chulainn.**

them: Fraech had found a new home with the Sídhe. Somehow, it seemed, that with his death their obligation to Cú Chulainn's challenge had been met: driving his chariot at full gallop, Fergus mac Róich was now able to clear the tree with ease.

Grim Comedy

In the days that followed, more of Connacht's finest warriors were sent out to tackle Cú Chulainn; one by one they were vanquished and killed. Medb, already irked at what she saw as her men's failure, flew into a rage when the "Hound" of Ulster killed her hound, Baiscne. He had been a favourite pet of Connacht's queen: seeing him loping across the landscape in the distance, Cú Chulainn had whirled his sling and sent a stone to take his head clean off. More men were sent out to their deaths, the tragedy turning briefly into farce when Cú Chulainn found a charioteer working on a broken shaft and assumed he was from Ulster. (He was in fact the slave of Orlám, a royal prince of Connacht and the favourite son of Ailill and Medb.) The charioteer in his turn had no inkling of who he was speaking to: he matily asked Cú Chulainn to help him trim some wood for his

BELOW: Slieve Foy, in Co. Louth: Cú Chulainn reputedly saw off a succession of Connacht heroes in single combat here.

repair. Cú Chulainn pitched in cheerfully: they chatted as they worked, the hero expressing his surprise that an Ulsterman's chariot was in so exposed a position with the enemy so close by. Asked how the vehicle had been damaged, the charioteer replied that it had been smashed trying to catch Cú Chulainn.

Only then did the two men realize the mistake that both had made. Cú Chulainn told the other not to fear for his own life: he had no quarrel with chariot drivers. Finding that he served Orlám, though, he made the man take him to his master. He quickly killed the prince, cut off his head and placed it on the charioteer's back, ordering him to carry it in that same position all the way back to the Connachtmen's camp to give to Orlám's parents. Cú Chulainn would be watching to make sure that he complied, and would kill him with his sling if he disobeyed.

In the event, the king and queen were walking outside the enclosure when he arrived: stopping there to share his news, the charioteer took the head from his back to show them. "Cú Chulainn said he'd kill me if I didn't carry your son's head in the same position all the way to our camp", he said, handing the head to them – even as a stone from the hero's sling hit his head and caused it to explode. Cú Chulainn, it seemed, expected his orders to be carried out absolutely to the letter: if he said "to the camp", he didn't mean outside it ….

Collateral Damage

Cú Chulainn swore to himself that he would take a shot with his sling every time he so much as saw Ailill or Medb. That meant some reckless shots in the days that followed, taken on the instant at disadvantageous distances: two of Medb's dearest pets were to pay the price. One was a little squirrel she was accustomed to carry with her on her shoulder – its head was torn

ABOVE: **Cú Chulainn's death became emblematic of a modern, nationalist "Celtic Revival" in this famous sculpture by Oliver Sheppard, 1911.**

off by a shot intended for its mistress. Next to bear the brunt was a bird that rode around with her, clinging to her shapely neck: it was smashed by another stone and killed. (Medb's animal companions strike an oddly maternal, nurturing note in the myth's depiction of a woman whose femininity is generally more of the seductive, sinister and destructive kind, but they remind us of her probable origins as an earth-goddess.) Human casualties inevitably followed: sons of Ailill and his closest courtiers were killed by missiles aimed by Cú Chulainn and the king. More men were to die in the days that followed.

ABOVE: In Stephen Reid's representation, the raven of ill-omen comes to warn a characteristically unintimidated Cú Chulainn of impending death.

A Visit from the Morrigan

At this point, another bird appears in the story, this one less engaging than the one that Medb had until recently carried with her as a pet. In the field in which it grazed in Cooley, the big brown bull Donn Cuailnge one day looked up to see a big black raven flutter down and alight upon a standing stone. It was, of course, the Morrigan, and she brought a warning to the bull of the sort of carnage so soon to be carried out in his name. "Dark bull, do you grow uneasy?", she asked:

Do you sense that they're all assembling
For the slaughter? Enemies swarm over
The beautiful green fields of Ulster.
Grassy meadows wave like breeze-blown seas;
Fair flowers splash the scene with colour,
But on the open plain armies grind each other
Into dust.

As we've seen, the Morrigan could be threefold: the trio known as Morrigna. As Badb, she said, she'd soon be feeding fat from a field of gore. Such was the cycle of revenge that would follow this first bloodletting, she gloated, that there would be "eternal anger; endless deaths of kinsmen and of sons".

Startled, the great beast allowed himself to be herded by his handlers to the slopes of Sliab Cuilinn, an imposing mountain outside Newry, in Co. Armagh. As he went, excited young lads leapt on to his back to try to ride him but – in no mood to play – he shook them off impatiently. No fewer than 100 boys were killed this way as the bull charged through Cooley, his hoofs tearing out a trench across the country as he made his way. Meanwhile, Medb's army was pressing on more slowly, Medb and Ailill themselves lying low among their host so as not to be seen. Cú Chulainn, growing restive, loosed off a shot that killed Lochu, Medb's handmaiden, as she went down to a stream for water, momentarily mistaking the servant for her queen.

FERGUS AND FREUD

In some versions of the story, it is at about this point that Ailill and his lords become aware that neither Medb nor Fergus mac Róich are anywhere to be found in the Connachtmen's camp. Where could they be? And why would both be missing? It seems suspicious. Ailill sends his charioteer to look discreetly and, sure enough, he finds that Fergus and the queen have hung back behind the main body of the army to give themselves a little private time. They are, indeed, locked in a deep embrace and in a state of semi-undress: Fergus has removed his belt and his scabbard, laying it aside on the turf beside them. So intensely involved are they in their passion, neither notices Ailill's servant tiptoeing up close and stealing the sword from its sheath. Carrying it nervously back to his master, the man is surprised to find Ailill unsurprised and sanguine: Medb is just doing what it takes to keep an important ally onside, he says.

Not until much later, when their lovemaking is done, do Medb and Fergus clamber to their feet and look around – and only then does the disconcerted warrior realize that his sword is gone. He is reduced to going into a nearby wood, cutting down a branch and carving himself a sword of wood – but nobody is fooled, and on his return to camp he's roundly derided.

Medb's credentials as a castrating woman-monster have long since been well established in the *Táin Bó Cúailnge*: cynically seductive, she's beautiful but hard; cold, calculating and completely ruthless. And it doesn't take a psychoanalyst to see how the unfortunate Fergus is stripped of his symbolic manhood here – despite seemingly scoring a sexual coup. If we're assiduous enough, we can of course find hidden Freudian meanings in just about any narrative, but there's no doubt that such resonances are often disconcertingly close to the surface in Celtic myth. The Fergus of the Ulster Cycle is particularly interesting in his inconsistent treatment. Often unabashedly celebrated as one of Ireland's greatest heroes, he is, in fact, the very definition of manhood (the literal meaning, in Irish, of his name). He has, the story says, the strength of 700 men; it takes seven women at a time to satisfy him sexually; his battle-sword makes swishing arcs as long as any rainbow. Yet he's repeatedly and humiliatingly cut down to size – not just here but, as earlier, when he is first dethroned by Conchobar (actually, and more emasculatingly, by Conchobar's cunning mother), and when, after that, he's manipulated by the king into betraying Naoise.

Donn Cuailnge Cornered

In Ulster now, Medb's men went out attacking and pillaging.
They came back driving herds of cattle and leading strings of
slaves. Their queen was unimpressed, however: she had brought
them here with one object only, the securing of Donn Cuailnge,
and of that magnificent trophy she saw no sign. Among the
captives, though, was Lóthar, one of the animal's herdsmen, who
knew his charge of old: Medb asked him where he thought the
bull might be. "He left", the frightened man reported; set out for
the hills where he's hiding in the deep hollow called Dubchoire –
the "Black Cauldron" – in Glen Gat, below what's now Trumpet
Hill in Co. Louth. Medb sent Lóthar off with some of her men,
all armed with willow baskets to trap and capture the bull and
bring him back to her. But the bull, seeing Lóthar among those
who were trying to corral him, charged his old keeper, ripping
out his insides with his horns. Donn
Cuailnge galloped off and was lost to
view.

The River Rises

Approaching Cooley now, the forces
of Connacht had one last formidable obstacle to surmount: they
had to find a way of fording the River Cronn. It didn't help that,
as they drew close, the rushing torrent abruptly surged up to
meet them, doubling in depth and speed – or that Cú Chulainn
appeared brandishing his spear midstream. Maine went out to
meet him. The oldest of Medb and Ailill's sons knew he had a
special responsibility to show a lead. But Cú Chulainn quickly
slew him – as well as the 30 horsemen and 32 foot soldiers who
had come rushing up behind the prince to try to keep him safe.

From Slings to Single Combat

Cú Chulainn now retired from the river bank, content to sit
quietly atop a nearby mountain, casting the occasional desultory
stone down with his sling. Even so, as the hours and days passed,
he picked off dozens of warriors, then scores, then hundreds:
Connacht's army was being weakened by attrition. Ailill decided
that it was time to try to come to terms: he sent his friend Mac

OPPOSITE: **Fergus descends into Loch Rury, where he encounters a hideous river monster that causes his face to become twisted awry.**

THEY CAME BACK WITH HERDS OF CATTLE AND STRINGS OF SLAVES.

HERE WE STAND
HERE WE REMAIN

We simply want to take
our God ordained
place as indigenous
Ulster people.
Understanding and
living out our calling
We assume our identity
without shame.
Retaliation
Or indignation against
those who have
caused harm to our
Past, or castrate our
culture, our identity and
our place on this island

CUCHULAINN

ABOVE: **In the recent "Troubles", Protestant Loyalists claimed a Cú Chulainn who'd fought, not for all Ireland, but for Ulster.**

Roth to open negotiations with the hero. He could have the noblest of the Ulster women they had captured and the finest of the livestock they had taken if he'd stop slinging stones – he could kill as many as he wanted in regular combat during the day. Cú Chulainn refused: he would, however, agree to cease with his sling if the Connachtmen would put up one man a day to face him in single combat. Ailill agreed – even though he fully concurred with Fergus' suspicion that Cú Chulainn was simply trying to spin things out until his fellow Ulstermen got past their phantom labour pangs. What alternative did they have?, he reasoned. It was better to lose one man a day than dozens, regularly picked off by Cú Chulainn's sling.

The young Etarcomol couldn't wait to be the first of Connacht's champions to face down Ulster's hero – even though Cú Chulainn had told Fergus he would spare him for his friendship's sake. Etarcomol insisted on fighting, though, and, as he hurtled into combat in his chariot, Cú Chulainn tried to warn the youth of the danger he was playing with, effortlessly slitting open his tunic with his sword as he flew by. But Etarcomol came in for another pass: this time Cú Chulainn made his message clearer – whirling his sword above his head, he neatly shaved off Etarcomol's crown. This only served to provoke the young man: this time, as he charged up in his chariot to kill Cú Chulainn, the Ulsterman swung his sword down on his skull and split him all the way to his navel.

Fight or Flight?

Possibly Connacht's most famous warrior, Nadcranntail knew he'd be doing well to vanquish Cú Chulainn by sheer strength of arms, so he decided to use cunning. He fashioned for himself nine spears from sharpened holly boughs. When he got to the ford where Cú Chulainn was waiting he found him idly jumping up to pluck flying birds down from the sky. One by one, Nadcranntail sent his own spears flying across the water at the hero: he, unfazed, simply caught those too as they whizzed by. But he was sufficiently distracted by the time the ninth spear reached him that the flock of birds he'd been bent on catching managed to make its escape over the other bank: running after them as they flew, Cú Chulainn appeared to be in a coward's flight.

CÚ CHULAINN APPEARED TO BE IN A COWARD'S FLIGHT.

Rejoicing at this outcome, Medb and the men of Connacht jeered to see the great champion of Ulster being so easily defeated. Cú Chulainn was put out, of course: he had never thought of fleeing, simply deciding to carry on with his bird hunt once it had become apparent that Nadcranntail had flung all nine of his spears in vain. He demanded a rematch and Nadcranntail, although convinced that to fight such a coward as Cú Chulainn had appeared to be would now demean him, couldn't reasonably refuse the Ulsterman's request. The next day it took place, the two men agreeing the rules before they began fighting: they'd throw spears at each other, and weren't allowed to dodge – except by jumping vertically. Nadcranntail hurled his spear, which scudded swift and true through the morning air, but Cú Chulainn nimbly leapt to avoid it and

HELL HATH NO FURY...

A beautiful young princess appeared before Cú Chulainn after his victory against Nadcranntail. She was richly dressed and came with cattle and gifts. She had, she said, heard much of him, of his handsomeness, strength and warlike prowess, and all she'd heard had made her fall in love with him. Cú Chulainn dismissed her impatiently: this was a busy time and he wasn't here to meet a

woman; she should be on her way as he had more important things on his mind. He had no idea that he was actually talking to the Morrigan in one of her less menacing guises – although still as dangerous as ever, however attractively she presented. "I've been behind you", she objected, "all this time. Who do you think has been standing with you, supporting you? Well, if you don't want my love you can always have my hatred." She would, she swore, stop at nothing, take on every form she could to frustrate him from now on: she'd become an eel to trip him as he forded a river; turn into a she-wolf to stampede cattle at him.

The Morrigan was as good as her word – or as bad as it – but Cú Chulainn remained unfazed. One day she took the shape of a heifer and charged at him with all her herd. Although she had her spirits hold him down while she attacked, he managed to reach his sling and unleash a stone: one of her eyes was shattered, leaving her still more furious than before.

ABOVE: **The Morrigan appeared before Cú Chulainn as a beautiful princess.**

it smashed itself against a standing stone. As Cú Chulainn's shaft hissed through the air, Nadcranntail tried to do the same, but his opponent had aimed high and his spear drove straight through Nadcranntail's head.

A tough and seasoned soldier, Nadcranntail – although transfixed by the spear – had not been killed, but he knew that if the weapon were removed his life would leave him. After an agreed pause, the two men returned to the fray: Nadcranntail staggered forward and flung his sword at Cú Chulainn's body, but the Hound was once again able to spring up to safety as it whizzed below his feet. Provoked beyond endurance now, however, he leapt again – this time at Nadcranntail's shield: clambering on to it, he swung with his sword and beheaded him. His bloodthirst still not sated, he whirled his sword again and cleaved the wretch's body all the way down the middle, from neck to navel.

HE WHIRLED HIS SWORD AGAIN AND CLEAVED THE WRETCH'S BODY.

Meanwhile, Medb, with a small advance guard, had found her way deep into Ulster and found the great bull Donn Cuailnge she had so long sought. Fergaimen, its loyal herdsmen, tried hard to protect his charge, but Medb stampeded his herd and he was crushed into the ground. So, Medb had won what she had come for, but it was not so easy to call off a war with so much honour at stake – and so many scores, both old and new, now to be settled. In a culture of pride and personal revenge, war can very quickly become self-perpetuating: certainly, there was no way for Ailill and Medb to withdraw from the conflict they had started now.

Slowly Drained

More Connachtmen came forward to meet Cú Chulainn in single combat, and more were defeated, and mostly killed – all, indeed, except Láréne. Cú Chulainn clutched his body so hard and pitched him up and down so violently that his bowels were completely crushed, filling the air around with an appalling stench. Despite the distinction of being the only warrior ever to survive a bout with Ulster's hero, Láréne spent the rest of his life in dismal embarrassment and pain.

Unvanquishable he might be, but Cú Chulainn was sufficiently mortal to find this day in, day out routine of heroics taxing. Over time, he started to feel seriously tired – especially once, having made an enemy of the Morrigan, he had to contend with her aggression too. Still, there was no let-up: Medb and Ailill appealed for talks, but the meeting they got Cú Chulainn to agree to turned out to be a trap, an ambush, and he found himself fending off a hail of javelins. All in a day's work for the hero, perhaps, but slowly, steadily, he was wearying. Again, Medb and Ailill summoned him to a parley, but they sent a servant girl and the royal jester in their disguise. Cú Chulainn, not fooled for a moment, set them up, impaled atop tall standing stones, a motley King and Queen of Connacht exposed to general ridicule.

At this point, Medb decided that the agreement they'd made earlier to send men at Cú Chulainn singly must be broken: they couldn't afford this daily toll upon their finest warriors. (She forgot that this pact had first been made at their request, to spare their forces.) All of a sudden, Cú Chulainn found himself

BELOW: Medb is believed to have been buried on Knocknarea, County Sligo. A prehistoric cairn is supposed to be her grave.

fighting off the entire army of Connacht, with its allied forces from Ireland's other kingdoms. A volley of 14 spears came at him in a moment but Cú Chulainn casually handed them off as they closed in on him; next, 100 warriors engaged him at the same time by a river crossing. They were all killed, and so easily that Medb denounced it as sheer murder: the place was referred to as Cét Chuile, "The Crime of a Hundred", from that time on.

CÚ CHULAINN SAW THE GLOWING SKY TINGED GOLD AND BRONZE FROM THE GLINT OF WEAPONRY.

Medb called in more favours, made more threats, and in the days that followed a mighty army massed along Ulster's edge, with warriors from all the length and breadth of Ireland. Looking out at sunset, Cú Chulainn saw the glowing sky tinged gold and bronze from the glint of weaponry to the far horizon: rather than intimidated, though, he was utterly enraged. Flying into a fit of violent anger, he grabbed swords and shields by the handful and yelled so loud that all the devils and goblins in the world joined in. The very sound was enough to set the enemy shaking – over a hundred fighters fell dead from sheer fright.

A Welcome Rest

But Cú Chulainn was not growing any less tired. As he stood there, swaying in his weariness, he saw a single warrior walking towards him from the north. Assuming it was another champion sent to face him, he braced and made ready to defend himself, but the man revealed that he had come in peace. He was not a man, in fact, but a soldier of the *Sídhe*, and for a great many centuries a god: he was known in tradition as long-armed Lugh, he said. He had seen the stand Cú Chulainn was taking and admired his courage and his strength, but he could see that he was tiring now and would like to help. Cú Chulainn, accordingly, lay down to sleep for three full days and nights, while Lugh stood guard for him. As the young man slept, Lugh treated his wounds with ointments and herbs.

Other allies were assembling, too. While Cú Chulainn slept, and while their fathers still writhed in pain, the boys of Ulster met together and agreed to come down with their hurling sticks

OPPOSITE: *Cú Chulainn hurtles into battle aboard his chariot, a terrifying sight.*

to help their hero. In all, 150 boys appeared and they fought bravely. They were finally cut down, but not before they'd killed three times their number of the enemy. Great deeds were done while Cú Chulainn took his rest.

Back to Battle

Waking up, Cú Chulainn was shocked and upset to find that he had been fast asleep for so long, concerned that the enemy should have been allowed to rest unscathed. When Lugh explained what he and the boys had done during his three-day break, he was reassured to know that the fight had continued, but he was filled with vengeful feelings at the Sons of Ulster's sacrifice. Asking his charioteer Laeg to make ready his sickle-wheeled chariot, he prepared himself to go into battle personally and make up for three days' and nights' lost time.

Cú Chulainn's chariot was equally a thing of beauty and of menace: the scythe-like blades protruding from the axle hubs were just the start. Sharpened hooks at every corner of the car made it a slashing, hacking hazard on every side; the horses that drew it wore mail coats, also bedecked with spikes. But the first and most important line of protection was the magic spell Laeg cast before putting the chariot in motion, making them invulnerable to attack – and invisible to the mortal eye. In the back, Cú Chulainn cut a frightening figure, armoured head to foot and armed

CÚ CHULAINN'S CHARIOT WAS EQUALLY A THING OF BEAUTY AND OF MENACE.

to the teeth, ready for action. Along with eight short swords, he wielded eight thrusting spears and the same number of javelins and shields. One on top of the other, 27 tunics covered his torso – not to protect it from spears and swords, but to ensure that, in his fighting frenzy, he didn't simply explode. His helmet, grooved and hollowed out, was an amplifying instrument, broadcasting his battle cry across the heavens for miles around.

Charging into action now, Cú Chulainn's body swelled with fury; his veins stood out throbbing violently and his sinews strained. Enemy warriors fell before him in their hundreds. The bloodlust high within him, he urged on Laeg, who took the chariot at a thundering gallop through the lines of the Connachtmen and

WHEELS OF WAR

The chariot was first used in the Middle East in around 3000 BC, so it certainly wasn't an invention of the Celts. They took to it with enthusiasm, though – Julius Caesar described encountering them on his campaigns both in Gaul and Britain – and it really isn't difficult to see why. The chariot was not just a weapon of war. It wasn't even a weapon of war, some scholars have suggested, although this is harsh: in certain circumstances, a crashing chariot-charge could demoralize and disperse an untrained and undisciplined enemy. There's something in what the sceptics say, though, and it's true that the ancient Romans, for example, used the chariot mainly as a ceremonial platform on which a victorious general could be publicly paraded – much like the open-topped limousine in which a modern world leader might be driven.

In the context of the sort of wars the Romans fought, the chariot had little use – except in triumphs of this kind (or, of course, in the Colosseum for races). But for warrior cultures like the Celts', and those of Homer's heroes, the chariot was naturally a vehicle of choice. To some extent, for such cultures warfare was in any case semi-ceremonial; a stylized ritual of personal challenge, prowess and combat between individual warriors.

As for the sickle-wheeled chariot, that is one of those things that, while widely described in the ancient sources, hasn't really cropped up in archeological investigations down the years. Its appeal is obvious: blazing into battle and scattering soldiers like harvested wheat, it would cut a satisfying swathe through the most formidable enemy. Some experts have, however, wondered whether this extraordinary machine of war ever actually existed – it is possible that it was little more than an ancient techno-fantasy, similar to James Bond's customized Aston Martin in the modern day.

their allies where they were thickest; great heroes fell, like fields of corn at harvest time. That day, 130 kings were killed, say the chroniclers: the other casualties were uncountable, although Cú Chulainn and his chariot came through without a scratch.

The Fight with Ferdia

At their wits' end by now, Ailill and Medb cast about for another champion to challenge Cú Chulainn. Finally, they thought of Ferdia. Not only was he protected by his uniquely horny skin, he had trained in arms with Cú Chulainn's own teacher, Scáthach. The only skill she hadn't taught him was how to use the *Gáe Bolg*: this was Cú Chulainn's favourite weapon, but he didn't have the bony carapace around his body that Ferdia did.

Even so, Ferdia was wary when he was summoned to see Medb and Ailill. He saw no reason to fight a fellow student of Scáthach's, whom he looked on as a friend. Since his father Damán had been among those who'd helped to look after the young Sétanta, he was pretty much a foster-brother to Cú Chulainn. The offer of Finnabair, Princess of Connacht, as his wife could not sway him, lovely though she was; nor could the promise of a passionate night with Queen Medb herself. In the end, what persuaded him to agree was Medb's cunning hint that Cú Chulainn had slighted his courage and his prowess: hearing this, he agreed to the combat instantly.

GREAT HEROES FELL, LIKE FIELDS OF CORN AT HARVEST TIME.

When battle was finally joined, the contest could not have been closer: the heroes repeated warlike drills they'd learned together at Scáthach's school in Skye. They fought with darts, javelins, short swords and sharp-edged shields; they thrust at each other with pikes and swung at one another with big broadswords. When a whole day's non-stop sparring had failed to yield any result, they stopped for the night, resting before resuming at dawn. That second day brought them no closer to a clear outcome. Again they rested, believing that the third day would decide the battle. For several hours it appeared that even now no winner would emerge from the melee of stabbing, slashing, thrusting, swinging and gouging, but at the last Cú Chulainn

Finnabair Fatale

Medb's offer of her daughter Finnabair to Ferdia is entirely in keeping with the general attitude taken towards women and female sexuality in the *Táin Bó Cúailnge*. The queen herself isn't slow to use her (seemingly considerable) allure, as we've seen – nor, for that matter, does her husband Ailill seem to judge her. Their daughter also doesn't obviously object to her mother's deployment of her beauty as a bargaining counter. (Indeed, when she's asked to seduce Rochad mac Faithemann, one of Ulster's foremost warriors, and buy his collaboration with Connacht, she jumps at the chance of bedding a man whom she adores.)

But Finnabair, it becomes clear, is by no means completely without a conscience. Connacht's campaign against Ulster eventually grinds to a halt when it becomes apparent to the allied Irish rulers that every single one of them has secretly been promised Finnabair. When a battle-royal results and 700 brave men are killed, Finnabair immediately falls dead with shame.

reached discreetly for his *Gáe Bolg* and caught it firm in the grasp of one hand even as, in the other, he raised his thrusting spear to strike. Ferdia raised his shield and, as he did so, Cú Chulainn stooped low and swung beneath his tunic to ram the *Gáe Bolg* up his backside. He knew how tough his opponent's bone-hide was and how hopeless it would be to try to penetrate it: this was the only way through to his vital organs, Cú Chulainn realized. Ferdia fell, and as he did so, his killer's sense of triumph and relief gave way to grief, for he remembered how close their brotherhood had been in times gone by. Áth Ferdiad, "Ferdiad's Ford", the spot where the fight took place was thenceforth called. Over time, that name was shortened to "Ardee".

Ulster in Action

While Cú Chulainn recuperated from his wounds, things were starting to happen further north. Only now were the men of Ulster shaking off their "labour" pangs. They mobilized at Emain Macha and marched south in their tens of thousands, Conchobar before them, ready at long last to engage the enemy. Ulster's king

OPPOSITE: **Fateful friendship. In Ernest Wallcousins' (1905) representation, Cú Chulainn carries Ferdia's body across the ford.**

summoned Ailill to a meeting, and the men agreed that they would do battle. Next day, the dawn was welcomed by the ghastly figure of the Morrigan, acclaiming the day on which she'd see "ravens chewing at the skin of men's necks, blood gushing out … carved-up flesh and battle frenzy". Gleefully impartial, she ended with the complicated cry:

Long live Ulster!
Down with Ireland!
Down with Ulster!
Long live Ireland!

She was to have her way: both sides would win and both would lose when the climactic battle was joined a few hours later. In their tens of thousands, Ireland's bravest warriors clashed. Great deeds were done: with one stroke of his sword, Fergus in his fury took the tops off three adjacent hills; Medb herself led a charge that came close to breaking through. Connacht was carrying the day, indeed, the warriors of Ulster were on the point of despairing when Cú Chulainn joined the fray and turned the tables. By the time he was finished, the forces of Connacht were finished too, fleeing in disorder from a field deep with their dead.

But Medb was to have one final triumph before she fled the field. Cú Chulainn himself, it's said, though invincible in the face of any normal foe, was in the end defenceless against her machinations. She persuaded Lugaid mac Con Roí, whose father Cú Chulainn had killed, to fling three enchanted spears: the first at Cú Chulainn's charioteer; the second at his peerless horse, bringing his car to an unceremonious stop; then he hurled the third into the hero's belly, spilling all his innards. Even then, Cú Chulainn refused to fall, tying himself to a standing stone so he might remain upright himself, until the treacherous Lugaid at last dispatched him with a poisoned sword.

Ulster's triumph was tempered twice over: not only had her greatest hero effectively been assassinated, but there was the ignominy of having lost the great brown bull. For Donn Cuailnge was being herded before the Connacht army as it went. Connacht's warriors might have won the war, but they'd lost the thing it had been fought for, a further ironic twist in what should have been a heroic tale. And more of these are to follow, for no sooner do Medb and Ailill get back to Cruachan with their Brown Bull of Cooley than he meets the great White-faced Bull, Finnenbach Ai. They fight and, although Donn Cuailnge wins and kills his opponent, he is fatally wounded himself. Rampaging around all of Ireland in his agony, he tears up the country, throwing up hills and gouging out valleys before he dies.

So the final reckoning for the war leaves countless thousands dead, and no one really victorious. This "cattle raid" has left both sides losing one bull. All a tragic waste? So the modern reader sees it, certainly. It is by no means clear, though, that this interpretation would have been available to those first audiences who listened as these stories were resoundingly recited by Celtic bards. Slight as the cause may have been, the deeds of bravery and honour they occasioned were genuinely epic.

THE RITUAL OF WAR

That Conchobar's first action on coming into contact with his enemy is to hold a parley, agree a truce and formally arrange for a battle to be fought later, underscores what seems to us the ritualistic quality of Celtic warfare. This quality is constantly being underlined in the text of the *Táin Bó Cúailnge*, in which even full pitched battles tend to be narrated as successions of single-combat scenes. Ailill's speech, calling on his heroes of Connacht to prepare themselves for action as Ulster's army approaches, is, in Thomas Kinsella's 1969 translation, a veritable poem of proper names:

Rise up, Traigthrén, swift-footed. Summon for me the three called Conaire from Sliab Mis; the three fair ones called Les, in Luachair; the three called Meid from Corpthe Loste; the three named Buidir from the River Buas; the three called Badb from the River Buaidnech; the three called Buaideltach from the River Berba; the three Muredachs from Marga; the three Laegaires from Lec Derg …

Individual pride; local patriotism: these trump anything we might call a wider "national" interest in the Celtic ethos. Although called a king and queen, Ailill and Medb might be better viewed as leaders of a loose alliance: the limits of their "kingdom" of Connacht are vague and ill-defined. By the same token, indeed, as convenient as the shorthand is, it's strictly speaking anachronistic to refer to a force like theirs or Ulster's as an "army". At least, it is if we expect this to mean the sort of carefully ordered, co-ordinated and regimented mass of men (and, these days, women) we are likely to see engaged in a modern war.

THE FENIAN CYCLE

Thought to be of later origin than the stories of the *Táin Bó Cúailnge*, the stories of the so-called "Fenian Cycle" evoke a world in which the warrior tradition meshes more obviously with one of mystery and magic.

A thousand years of history have pushed Ireland and Scotland further apart: it can be a shock to see the map showing the narrowness of the North Channel between the two. In ancient times, as we've already seen, the traffic between them was busy – and for the most part easy – and the people of both countries felt a clear Celtic kinship. Whether formally connected (as they were for a while by the kingdom of Dál Riata), or more loosely (as when Cú Chulainn went to train on Skye with Scáthach), the two nations had much in common, culturally, linguistically, in their modes of life – and also, of course, in their stock of stories. Fionn mac Cumhaill, for example, is as much a part of Scottish as of Irish myth. But he didn't just straddle the strait between the

OPPOSITE: **In one version of his story, Fionn's first marriage was to Tasha, princess of the *Sídhe*.**

two countries. In some stories he is depicted as a giant, and could quite literally stand astride the North Channel: this is the Fionn mac Cumhaill who built Antrim's Giant's Causeway and hurled the Isle of Man into the Irish Sea, leaving the giant hollow that became Lough Neagh. This outsized, semi-comic Fionn may on the one hand be seen as a modern burlesquing of the older, more heroic tradition – or, on the other, it may provide a connection back to a still more ancient age in which mythic Ireland and Scotland were populated by giants (themselves, perhaps, recast from remembered pagan gods). But, as with just about every other area of Celtic cultural tradition, boundaries appear to be there to be breached. Certainly, in the stories of what's known as the "Fenian Cycle", Fionn bridges the divide between the life of mortals and the supernatural – and, in some ways, between the ancient and the modern worlds.

The Outsider

Fionn mac Cumhaill was to prove by far the most modern of mythic heroes. He and his warriors – the *Fianna* – were always outsiders, rebels. It was, to be sure, an extravagantly romantic flight that saw a small group of anti-British revolutionaries in the nineteenth century name themselves "Fenians" – but there's no doubt that the label made a sort of sense. Like Cú Chulainn before him, Fionn mac Cumhaill had the title by which we know him bestowed on him as a nickname: born Deimne, he was called "Fionn" (meaning "fair" or

"white") for his blond hair. His mother, Muirne, was a druid's daughter, celebrated for her beauty, much admired and assiduously courted, although she rebuffed all such attentions out of hand. One man, Cumhaill, the leader of a group of landless, lordless warriors (semi-brigands might be a better description) called the *Fianna*, was not prepared to take no for an answer. He kidnapped Muirne and took her away by force. Licensed by Conn, High King of Ireland, her father's friends set out in hot pursuit: it wasn't long before they'd caught Cumhaill and killed him. By that time, though, he'd already raped the maiden he'd decided would be his bride.

Muirne was left pregnant, her reputation ruined: victim or not, she would from now on be damaged goods. Cast out from her community, she was welcomed by Bodhmail, a druidess – and, as it happens, the sister of Cumhaill. Her brother's killer, Goll mac Morna, had been his second-in-command and rival in the *Fianna*: it seemed unlikely he would want to leave a son

Bag of Tricks

Like so many figures in the "Fenian Cycle", Cumhaill had a foot in both the real and the supernatural worlds: the opposition finds a sort of polarity in him. A bullying and vicious thug, a robber and a rapist, he also had a special otherworldly aura, most obviously symbolized in the fact that he had keeping of the *Fianna*'s famous "Treasure Bag". Magically made in crane skin, this bag was full of special weapons that could save the carrier in just about any conceivable tight corner. Although it was taken by Lia after Cumhaill's death, Fionn's first act on leaving Bodhmail and Liath Luachra's home on the forest was to retrieve it. Fate contrived that he should meet Lia as he set out upon his road: they fought and Fionn took his father's treasure back.

ABOVE: **For illustrator Arthur Rackham (1920), the young Fionn was very much a child of nature.**

of Cumhaill's alive to exact revenge on his behalf. Fortunately, Bodhmail had an isolated home deep in a wooded valley in the Slieve Bloom Mountains, located in the very heart of Ireland. Muirne was able to rest there undisturbed while the weeks and months went by. When at last she bore a son she named him Deimne and left him in Bodhmail's care. The druidess became one of his two foster-mothers. The other, her companion Liath Luachra, was a famous warrior woman: what Scáthach had done for Cú Chulainn, she did for Deimne. Or for Fionn as this tall and brave young boy was now coming to be called, from the shock of fair hair that made the sight of him so arresting.

Fionn's mother, meanwhile, had found herself a husband and protector in the King of Munster. It seemed safe now for her to come back and fetch her son. But Bodhmail and Liath Luachra wouldn't let her have him. As far as they were concerned, the path and purpose of Fionn's life was irrevocably ordained: he was to be an avenger for his father and

AS FINNEGAS' SERVANT, FIONN HAD THE JOB OF PREPARING THE SALMON OF KNOWLEDGE FOR HIS MASTER.

Bodhmail's brother. Cumhaill's crime against Muirne couldn't detract in any way from the sacred duty of a son to stand behind the man who sired him. The boy's whole identity was as "Fionn mac Cumhaill" – Fionn, Cumhaill's Son. He was still only seven

FAMILY VALUES?

The relationship between Bodhmail and Liath Luachra in the legend hasn't escaped notice in the recent debate in Ireland over questions of gay adoption and gay marriage. The old texts don't go into detail as to what the Druidess and her warrior companion did in bed, but they do make it clear that theirs was a long and close relationship, and that they were partners in Fionn's upbringing as in all else. While Bodhmail took charge of traditionally "feminine" qualities, training him to feel and sympathize and to express himself in poetry, Liath Luachra gave him his education in physical fitness and the more "manly" military arts.

The prejudice against male homosexuality as intrinsically unmanly is arguably itself a product of less tough modern times: ancient warrior cultures all seem to have gone in for a great deal of what might very loosely be called "male bonding". The Celts were no exception. As notorious as "Greek love" might be now, writers like Aristotle commented in some surprise about the extent to which sexual relationships between men were accepted – even honoured – in Celtic culture. Some degree of ambiguity is inevitable, of course: the arduousness and danger of soldiering makes for an intense connection between comrades – at what point do we start to see this sort of closeness as something more? In some sources, the relationship between Cú Chulainn and Ferdia is seen as simply friendship; in others, their final fight to the death draws a special quality of pathos from the suggestion that their connection was actually much closer.

That said, the relationship between Bodhmail and Liath Luachra doesn't ultimately undermine the values of the "patriarchy": on the contrary, when Muirne comes to take Fionn back his foster-mothers send her packing. The most important thing for Fionn, they firmly agree, is that he fulfils his responsibilities to his father by taking vengeance for his death – however unworthy Cumhaill may have proved to be.

when Liath Luachra decided she'd taught him all she could: now he had to go out into the world and complete his training through experience. As young as he was, he already had more than a man's strength and surpassing skill and courage: it was time for him to tackle the world and its hazards on his own.

The Salmon of Knowledge

So strong and accomplished a boy should have had no difficulty finding a lord to serve, and so it proved – until, each time, Fionn's parentage emerged. No chief, whatever his prestige and power, fancied falling foul of Goll mac Morna: Fionn was reluctantly but invariably let go. Wandering further and further afield to seek a place, the young Fionn found himself beside the River Boyne where he met the elderly druid Finnegas. Dedicating his whole life to the search for knowledge and understanding, Finnegas had spent years in the attempt to catch the so-called Salmon of Knowledge, which was believed to inhabit this stretch of water. Having eaten the hazelnuts that had fallen into the stream from the sacred trees along the bank (like those in the story of Boann's well), this miraculous fish had taken on all the knowledge and the wisdom of the world. Whoever first tasted its flesh could expect to have all that insight for himself: Finnegas had resolved to be that man.

And he very nearly was. One day, to his triumph and delight, Finnegas caught the salmon

BELOW: As Finnegas' servant, Fionn had the job of preparing the Salmon of Knowledge for his master.

in the River Boyne. Lighting a fire to cook it on and mounting it upon a spit, he set his young attendant to turn it above the flames. He did so, and as the minutes passed the salmon gradually began to cook: soon its scales were starting to hiss and bubble with the heat. Suddenly it spat, and Fionn felt his thumb seized with a searing pain: instantly, involuntarily, he shoved it in his mouth and sucked. At that point, he abruptly became possessed of all the knowledge and all the understanding in the world. Finnegas looked on, first in amazement and then in fury. From that time on, the druid knew, all the knowledge in the world belonged to the boy beside him – not to him, who had made its acquisition his life's work. And sure enough, thereafter, in his later life, any time Fionn mac Cumhaill felt confused or at a loss, he just had to bite his thumb to feel inspiration rushing in.

Tara's Halls

By tradition, Tara was the royal seat of the High Kings of Ireland. Modern archeology has been sceptical, to say the least. There's little evidence to support the idea that any such institution as a "High King" ever existed – and good grounds for suspecting that it was imaginatively imposed as a rationalization in retrospect. By early modern times, it seemed "natural" to think of Ireland as a

BELOW: The "Mound of the Hostages" is one of several prehistoric earthworks at Tara, traditional seat of Ireland's "High Kings".

SAMHAIN

If Lughnasadh welcomed in the harvest in all its plenitude, prosperity and promise, it could also be seen as signalling summer's passing. Civilizations since time began appear to have felt anxiety at the "death" of the year as represented in the dwindling of the day through summer's end and into autumn, but the joy of harvest has tended to keep these fears at bay. The Celts certainly appear to have succeeded in pushing such forebodings aside, at least until after the final completion of the harvest and the arrival of autumn proper. The festival of Samhain marked the coming of darkness and the end of life. Bonfires were lit to drive away the night, and offerings left out for ancestral spirits and the *Sídhe*. Samhain was held on the night of 31 October – in later Christian cultures, Halloween or All Saints' Eve. That festival too, of course, marks the passing of life and attempts to banish the fear of death through lively, macabre fun.

single entity, although for the ancient Celts all politics was local.

As with Rathcroghan and Fort Navan, we can't say too much for sure about the complex of earthworks and standing stones at Tara Hill in Co. Meath, except that it seems to have been a ceremonial site of some sort, constructed in the Iron Age (perhaps in part before). There are no real signs of serious fortifications or of major residential buildings – still less the imposing palace complex the legends ask us to imagine. What Tara does have to offer is an awe-inspiring setting and a haunting, evocative atmosphere: here the worlds of modernity and myth seem to connect.

On His Majesty's Service

Fionn now headed off across Ireland to Tara, to offer his services to the High King, Conn of the Hundred Battles, who lived there. Or rather, walking into the great hall in which the king and his warriors were gathered, he strode straight over and sat down in that company as though he were their oldest comrade. Asked to explain himself and his presence before the king, he did not flinch but stood up and calmly stated: "I am Fionn, son of Cumhaill. My father once served you, O King, and now I wish to serve you in my turn." Despite their difficult history (it had of course been Conn who'd authorized Fionn's father's killing for his crime against Muirne), the king appears to have taken to the boy.

Conn's experience and prestige as a warrior weren't in any doubt at all – hence his honorific, Conn "of the Hundred Battles". But despite this, he had to struggle to hold his head up as a king because of the repeated humiliations that had been inflicted on his reign. For two decades, a ghostly monster called Aillen the "Burner" would come across the threshold from the other world every year at Samhain, emerging out of his hillock in the open country some way to the south of Tara. Soaring high into the air, he'd swoop down, descending on the palace, setting it alight with his breath of flames and burning it to the ground. There was no resisting him because, as he first arrived on that evening, he'd lull the inhabitants to sleep with the softest, sweetest music they ever heard. The entire site would then be at his mercy.

Every year men armed to meet him; every year they awoke to find the mists of morning mingling with wisps of smoke from the scorched timbers and the blackened earth. The *Fianna* themselves had tried to defend their king's royal residence but, as tough and strong as they were as soldiers, they wilted weakly in the face of Aillen's song.

Fionn, however, had his treasure bag, held before by his father as the leader of the *Fianna*. He was perfectly equipped to deal with this emergency. Among the miscellaneous things in his bag was a spearhead that spontaneously glowed red-hot. As he sat up in preparation for that night's vigil, Fionn held the spearhead up before his brow: whenever he nodded, he pricked his forehead with the burning point and recoiled in pain. Aillen's song was ravishing indeed: it wafted over him, pulling at him like the charm it was, the ripple of his harp blending with the mellifluous notes of his pipe and the crooning of his soft, soft voice. Fionn couldn't help it: he teetered over into enraptured drowsiness. No sooner than he did, however, than he was jolted awake by the shock of so much pain: he rubbed his eyes, shook himself awake and renewed his guard. A distinctly unpleasant night, then, but his discomfort saved his consciousness: when Aillen came in for his attack, Fionn was ready for him.

Seeing him standing there, his sword raised, Aillen swooped down, shooting out a gust of flame, but Fionn raised up his red cloak and it helped to shield him from the heat. And that was just about it: the spirit hadn't been expecting anybody to be

ABOVE: "Fionn heard far off the first notes of the faery harp ..." But the red-hot spearhead helped him stay awake.

OPPOSITE: Blue-painted attendants take part in the Samhain Fire Festival in Edinburgh, Scotland.

awake, let alone fight back – still less to be able to withstand his breath of fire. Beaten, Aillen turned and fled, Fionn mac Cumhaill racing along in his fiery wake: just as he reached what must have seemed the safety of his mound, Fionn flung his spear.

THE FLYING GHOUL WAS SKEWERED BY THE SPEEDING POINT.

On his own doorstep, at the very threshold between this world and the other, the flying ghoul was skewered by the speeding point. At his leisure, Fionn walked up, swung his sword and cut off Aillen's head. Carrying this trophy back to (a still intact) Tara in triumph, Fionn was welcomed by the waking court and by King Conn. Goll mac Morna, acknowledging his greater claim, stepped aside to allow Fionn to head the *Fianna*.

If not specifically revenged, Fionn's father had at least been vindicated and his son was now leading in his place. Taking charge of the *Fianna*, Fionn set up a *dun* or stronghold on a volcanic outcrop in what is now Co. Kildare, towering above the eastern edge of the Bog of Allen.

Fionn a Father

One day when Fionn was hunting in the forest, his hounds caught and cornered a tiny fawn, but when he made as if to kill it they stopped him. Instead, capturing the frightened animal they carried it back to the camp with them. Suddenly, Fionn saw

RIGHT: Ben Bulben: Fionn is said to have hunted on its slopes; W.B. Yeats was buried in its shadow (1939).

a beautiful, graceful lady in its place. Her name was Sadbh, the daughter of Derg Díanscothach, she explained, and she had been turned into a young deer by the Dark Druid, Fear Doirche, in his anger at her refusal to sleep with him. It seemed that so long as she was on Allen Hill where Fionn held spiritual sway she was able to remain in her human form. Should she leave it, she would once more become a fawn.

Staying with Fionn, she became his wife and they lived happily together until one day Fionn had to leave his fortress to deal with a military emergency. Sadbh, wretched without her husband, was beside herself with joy to see him returning early and she eagerly went with him when he suggested a walk outside. This "Fionn", however, was Fear Doirche in a magical disguise: as soon as she left the sanctuary of the Dun of Allen, Sadbh was turned into a fawn again. When the real Fionn returned, he hunted high and low for his beloved wife for weeks and months, but all in vain.

Seven years later, however, he stumbled on a naked child on the slopes of Ben Bulben, Co. Sligo: locals told him the boy had been seen being brought up in the nearby forest by a beautiful doe. He was, Fionn realized immediately, his own son, for so long lost and mourned for, and in his joy he named him Oisín or "Little Deer". In his father's loving care, Oisín was to grow up to be a mighty warrior – and, more famously, mythic Ireland's foremost poet.

ABOVE: **Fionn saved Sadbh from Fear Doirche, and she became his wife; eventually, though, the wicked sorcerer snatched her back.**

With Niamh to Neverland

The boundary between this world and the other is constantly being crossed in one direction or another in Celtic myth. In the "Fenian Cycle", it seems particularly porous. Perhaps the most striking visitor from the world beyond is the beautiful Niamh (or Neve). Her very name means "bright" or "shining", and she fully lives up to that in radiant looks.

One day, the story goes, Fionn and his warriors were out hunting in the forest when a woman on a horse appeared from out of the western sky. Seen close to, she was incomparable in her beauty and her grace, from her golden hair to her lovely skin and her dainty hands and feet. All the men were awestruck, but Fionn's son Oisín stood transfixed. Her name was Niamh, the lady said, and she had come to take Oisín with her to her home in the other world: it was, she told them, a land of eternal youth. Oisín begged his father to let him go: he promised he would come back and visit him very soon. Despite a sense of foreboding, Fionn didn't feel he could refuse.

BELOW: **Niamh spirits Oisín away to the world of the *Sídhe* on her snow-white horse.**

So Oisín climbed up on to the horse's back behind Niamh and off they galloped, soaring high among the clouds. Oisín was literally transported by his passion, swept away. And why not? No sinister or duplicitous spirit, Niamh was to give him everything she had promised: all her beauty; all her loyalty; all her love. Her home country too was all she had said it would be, a place of ceaseless sunshine, carefree happiness and endless youth.

Even so, the first ties are always strong and, for all his happiness, after three years Oisín found he was pining for at least a sight of his father Fionn and his old friends. Niamh was concerned to see this restless stirring, but still she did not want to discourage what she knew were legitimate feelings nor to do anything to stand in the way of his happiness. At last, then, she agreed to let him borrow her magic horse so that he could ride back and see his native home in Ireland. He would, though, find it a great deal changed; nor

HE WAS SURPRISED AND PROFOUNDLY SHOCKED BY WHAT HE SAW.

should he be too disappointed if he didn't get the welcome he was anticipating, Niamh warned. And whatever he did, he must remember that, while it was fine to see his country he was on no account to set foot in it: that would sever the tie that connected him with this other world – and her.

Oisín was too excited at the prospect of seeing his home country to absorb these warnings, but he was surprised and profoundly shocked by what he saw. Niamh's country was indeed a land of eternal youth: it followed that the three years he'd passed there had represented 300 in the time of mortal humans. Fionn and all the rest of his family and friends had long since died, and Ireland had changed beyond recognition. When he asked about the people he knew, he found that, while their names were clearly known, they endured only as legendary figures from long-bygone times. Sadly, Oisín turned to go, but before he did he jumped down to take a drink from a stream – forgetting for a moment the strict prohibition Niamh had made.

The moment he came into contact with the earth, he became a mortal man and his time caught up with him: suddenly, he was a bent and wizened man on the brink of death. (In some sources, he's found and tended in his sickness by St Patrick, newly arrived on his mission to Ireland – but no miracle healing is to be worked.) By the time an anxious Niamh, now the mother of Oisín's child, could come across herself to search for him, he was dead and nowhere to be found.

ABOVE: Once he made contact with the ground, Oisín became a mortal man again: in an instant, he aged 300 years.

THE OSSIAN IMPOSTURE

Fionn mac Cumhaill's place in Irish tradition is assured. His status
in Scotland is less secure – in some considerable part, ironically,
because of former fame. When, in the eighteenth century, the poet
and scholar James Macpherson (1736–96, *right*) decided to confect
his own "ancient" Gaelic bard, he chose to adopt the persona of
Fionn's son Oisín – or "Ossian", as he modernized the name. Ossian
was supposedly the legendary poet himself, the son of the mythic
hero Fionn or "Fingal". Macpherson maintained that a series of
poetic fragments he started publishing in 1760 (*below*) had been
taken directly from original Gaelic manuscript sources that he had
discovered: he himself had been no more than their translator. And
Macpherson was indeed a Gaelic scholar of proven distinction:
nothing in his claim was inherently implausible.

But there was something about the work of Ossian that seemed
too good – even too Gaelic – to be true. This was just how a proud
and noble Celtic bard might have been expected to have written –
perhaps suspiciously so:

> As the dark shades of autumn fly over the hills of grass; so
> gloomy, dark, successive came the chiefs of Lochlin's ecchoing
> woods. Tall as the stag of Morven moved on the king of groves.
> His shining shield is on his side like a flame on the heath at night.
> When the world is silent and dark, and the traveller sees some
> ghost sporting in the beam.

Dr Johnson saw straight through Macpherson's claims: the poems of
Ossian weren't just rubbish, he said, but a "gross imposition" on the
reading public. But most readers were only too happy to be imposed
on. Even relatively sophisticated ones: Ossian's poems created a
sensation, sweeping Europe and North America, their fans including
U.S. President Thomas Jefferson and France's Napoleon Bonaparte. And it wasn't just the public:
composers like Felix Mendelssohn and Franz Schubert were to find inspiration in Ossian's works.
(The former's "Hebrides Overture", prompted by a visit to the so-called "Fingal's Cave" of Staffa, is a
reminder of the tourist boom the Ossian craze kicked off in Scotland.)

Yet the fact that those "taken in" by Macpherson's scam included such great poets as Johann
Wolfgang von Goethe calls into question how warranted Dr Johnson's contempt really was. The
poems may have been a pastiche, but they did partake of the originals' atmosphere and flavour, and
they found a way of bringing to life a remote romantic past. A readership tiring of classical correctness,
balance and order was looking to be carried away by wild rhetoric, untrammelled passion and
"primitive" feeling. For what it's worth, scholars today believe that Ossian's works were, at least in part,
based on original sources: it wasn't quite the wholesale fraud that has been claimed.

OPPOSITE: **Authentic or not, Ossian caught the continental imagination. His "Vision" was
captured by France's Ingres (1813).**

Crossed in Love

Years passed, and women came and went in the life of Ireland's strongest, most handsome hero. However, none since Sadbh could leave a strong impression on his heart. None, at least, until he saw Gráinne, the daughter of the High King Cormac mac Airt, and by general agreement the brightest beauty of her day. Fionn fell in love with her at first sight, and not unnaturally she was flattered to think that she had stirred such feelings in the heart of Ireland's greatest hero. Fionn asked Cormac for his daughter's hand and he was glad to give it. A great feast was held to celebrate their betrothal, and all of Ireland's brave warriors and fine ladies were there to show their support for their king, for his royal house, for Fionn and for what promised to be the most spectacular match the country had seen in many years.

A GREAT FEAST WAS HELD TO CELEBRATE THEIR BETROTHAL.

Among the guests was Diarmuid Ua Duibhne, the son of Donn, in older Irish tradition a semi-divinity with a role as lord of the dead. Whatever ironic overtones that parentage lends to his story, what mattered most immediately to Fionn was that he was a brave and extraordinarily handsome youth. Of more relevance, then, among Diarmuid's mythical antecedents, was the fact that, after his father's passing, he'd been fostered by Aengus, the old god of beauty, youth and love. And it certainly showed: in his face, his physique, his grace of movement, his easy manner and his gentle speech, it was hard to imagine a more attractive youth. (In one story, Diarmuid is accorded an allure that transcends all such real-world attractions: his irresistibility was actually magical, it suggests. One night in the woods, he met a woman of the *Sídhe* who, having once seduced him, had rewarded – or maybe cursed? – him with a love spot that made any woman who saw him fall instantly and obsessively in love.)

Whatever the source of his appeal, Gráinne could find no way of resisting it: as the feast went on, she made increasingly heavy weather of seeming to have eyes only for her intended husband. Indeed, she struggled to take her eyes off Diarmuid for so much as a moment. And no wonder, the women at the feast felt (although

they'd never voice the thought): not only was Diarmuid
extraordinarily striking in both his looks and bearing, he was
also a great deal closer to the bride-to-be in age. Diarmuid, in his
turn, could not look on Gráinne's beauty unmoved, but he was an
honourable man and he'd never think of offending against a man
he held in such high regard and respect as Fionn. Beside herself
with passion, however, Gráinne was lost to law and reason: she
had certain magical powers, and she used them now to cast a
spell. Diarmuid clearly loved her: whether he liked it or not,
then, she was going to make him give in to that feeling, put aside
all duty and all honour, and go off into the world to live with her.

All is Fair…

So the couple eloped, and although a furious Fionn set off with a party of supporters in hot pursuit, they managed to escape into the thickest of the forests. As Diarmuid's foster-father – and, of course, in his capacity as young love's patron and protector – Aengus helped them get away undetected and find a safe place to stay (said to have been a cave in Glenbeigh, Co. Kerry). Fionn's men pursued them there, but Diarmuid managed to fight them off and they had to return to the Dun of Allen empty-handed. The immediate crisis over, though, the fuss gradually died down. Aengus was even able to make a tactful approach to Fionn and talk him round. In the end, the hero let it be known that Gráinne and Diarmuid had his forgiveness. Their peace of mind restored, they got on with their lives together (and had five children, indeed) and over time became a comparatively ordinary family.

Aengus' overtures continued, and one day things were mended sufficiently for Fionn and Diarmuid to undertake a

BELOW: **Diarmuid and Gráinne's Cave, in the Glenliff Horseshoe, County Sligo, one of several hideouts in which the runaway couple stayed.**

MORAL SCRUTINY

Fionn's betrayal of the injured and dying Diarmuid was not his finest hour – although Fionn mac Cumhaill of course was never meant to be a modern gentleman: Celtic myths can be unpredictable that way. One moment they're reminding us with a jolt of just how little human nature has altered down the millennia; next, they're underlining how completely it's been modified by so many centuries of social change. It's easy enough to argue that the story makes psychological sense: Fionn's nobility was universally acknowledged; his reputation for fairness and courtesy unrivalled, but his feelings for Gráinne tested them to breaking-point – and some way beyond. And it wasn't just the loss of love, it was the loss of face as well – a huge humiliation for a man who, accustomed to nothing but admiration and respect, now felt like an object of pity and scorn. But to analyze his reactions in this way feels obviously anachronistic even as we do it: Fionn was who he was we just have to let him be.

hunting trip together. Friends again, they set out into the forest and had a wonderful morning's sport, until – all of a sudden – Diarmuid was surprised by an angry boar. Before anyone could react, the animal had rushed out from the thicket in which the hounds had hemmed him and gored the young man with a wicked tusk. While their servants rallied round to help him, Fionn himself rushed off to a nearby spring: his enchanted hands would give this water healing powers. His first impulse may have been selfless, but as he ran Fionn seems to have started turning the situation over in his mind. Deep in his heart, it seems, he hadn't been able to get over his outrage at his treatment at the younger couple's hands all those years before. He had never quite stopped seething inwardly, despite himself. So while he ran to the spring as promised, and scooped up water in his hands, he took his time as he made his way back to where Diarmuid lay bleeding – and, some say, let the water that might have saved him trickle away between his fingers. Diarmuid died, and this meant that for Gráinne as well life was well and truly over – she pined away upon his grave. Fionn had finally exacted his revenge.

> HE HAD NEVER QUITE STOPPED SEETHING INWARDLY, DESPITE HIMSELF.

Complacent and Corrupt

Fionn's treatment of Diarmuid and Gráinne had already hinted that the "fair, white" hero had a much darker side. It seems that this became more evident as time went on. Under his leadership the *Fianna* grew, not just more powerful but – some said – more exacting, more entitled: they bullied kings and chiefs both for tribute and for influence. While Cormac mac Airt was High King, their overweening ways were tolerated, more or less – these two old men went back so far. But Cormac's son was not to prove quite so sentimental. Cairbre Lifechair wasn't ill-disposed to Fionn: in fact, he was his son-in-law, having married his younger daughter, Aine nic Fionn. They had a daughter together, Sgiam Sholais ("The Light of Beauty").

ABOVE: Old, and increasingly complacent, Fionn's *Fianna* were coming to be more a parasitic presence than a heroic one in Ireland.

The time came for Sgiam Sholais to be married and, as was often the custom in this period, this was seen as an opportunity for some informal diplomacy. Cairbre's sons – Sgiam Sholais' brothers – had killed King Aengus of the Déisi in the course of a quarrel.

Cairbre, concerned that the situation might spiral out of control and spark off a wider conflict, was eager for a way of smoothing things over. In the circumstances, it seemed the tactful thing to do to offer Sgiam Sholais to Aengus' son, Prince Maolsheachlainn: their marriage would create a bond of loyalty and peace between the families. The gesture was received in the conciliatory spirit in which it was intended, and plans were made for the young couple to wed.

At this point, though, the *Fianna* announced that they wanted 20 gold ingots by way of payment for "their" portion of the dowry that was to accompany the bride. If this idea struck Cairbre Lifechair as a little extraordinary, the alternative they offered was outrageous: that he should grant Fionn his first-night "right" of taking the virginity of the bride. (This prerogative passes without

LEFT: The baying of his
hounds fetched help
when, foolishly, Fionn
ventured into a cave
in which four hideous
witches dwelt.

comment when accorded to King Conchobar in the early pages of
the *Táin Bó Cúailnge* – a curiosity of what is apparently assumed
to have been a much remoter past.) That they should demand
so much – and with such bland assurance – drove the High King
into a fury. He sent a message to Fionn refusing both these things.
Fionn replied: rather than have the maidenhead, he'd have the
maiden's head – the *Fianna* would come and carry Sgiam Sholais
off to her execution.

The Road to Gabhra

Cairbre erupted: he determined to deal with the *Fianna* once
and for all and sent out his heralds to raise up an army across his
realm. To all of Ireland's kingdom they went: they found a ready
response from local kings and chiefs who had long since tired

RIGHT: **Conaran's daughters took Fionn and his friends captive – till rescuers were summoned by the barking of their hounds outside.**

of being pushed around by the *Fianna*. Quick to make common cause with Cairbre was Goll mac Morna, the disaffected former leader of the *Fianna*, and his group of like-minded malcontents. Soon great armies were massing, marching together to the banner of the High King Cairbre, converging on an area of hilly country south of Tara. For this was where the *Fianna* were assembling, having left their headquarters and slipped across the Bog of Allen, ready to respond to the High King and his allies on firmer ground, which they found on the lower slopes of Mount Gabhra. They stood there in seven battalions, sounding their battle horns in defiance of Cairbre, who was now advancing on them fast.

Then, says the battle chronicle, the *Cath Gabhra*, "these two vast forces came crashing together":

THESE TWO VAST FORCES CAME CRASHING TOGETHER.

"… and then was joined the Battle of Gabhra of the Hard Strokes – Ireland's greatest ever clash. The day was not yet old when the first heroic war-cries – or the first wailing from the wounded – were heard; the rending of shields; the hacking-off of heads; the opening up of gashes; the carving up of flesh; the gush of blood. It came cascading out on every side, trickling into every cranny of the ground beneath; the soldiers had to scramble over heaped-up carcases to make their way."

The *Fianna* were far outnumbered – 10- or 20-fold, some of the sources say – but they were outstanding warriors, and they had Oscur. Oisín's son – Fionn's grandson – was an army in himself. He cut a swathe through Cairbre's columns as they came on. He hurt the High King more directly when he took on both his beloved sons, Princes Conn and Art: swinging his sword, he beheaded them in turn before going off through the melee to find

BELOW: In Macpherson's Ossian epic, Fingal (Fionn) mourns his grandson's widow, Malvine, who dies while caring for the aged hero.

their father and kill him. But Cairbre quickly heard what Oscur had done: yelling in grief and rage, the king set off in search of him. The two men stalked each other over the battlefield. It was Cairbre who caught sight of his quarry first: with a grunt of anguished effort he unleashed his battle spear; it went right through Oscur's back, beneath the shoulder and into his heart. As the brave youth lay dying, his friends and kinsmen gathered round: it was the first time Fionn was ever seen to shed a tear.

Finale?

In some versions of the story it was also the last time Fionn did anything at all. Five of Cairbre's warriors – the Sons of Uigreann, whom Fionn had killed – closed in on the hero from behind as he knelt weeping beside his grandson's body, and they flung their spears at him. For many, though, Fionn never died: indeed, to this day he sleeps, along with his *Fianna*, in the heart of some green hill – perhaps underneath their old headquarters, the Dun of Allen. Here they've snoozed away the centuries, awaiting the call to arms that will waken them and summon them to save their country in its hour of greatest need. (That a country whose history has so notoriously been so tragic and conflict-ridden as Ireland's should still not apparently have reached that hour is a little worrying, it might be thought.) Even so, this makes a happy ending – fatuously so, perhaps: the image of a helpless hero caught unawares, unable to defend himself and being done to death by vindictive thugs seems somehow more realistic to the modern reader in its obvious ingloriousness, although it's every bit as much a mythic fantasy.

With all its seeming sentimentality, though, the story of the "Sleepers" is by no means entirely an unfitting one, given the importance of the otherworld in the "Fenian Cycle" as a whole. The thought of Fionn and his brave warriors, dreaming deep within their mountain, like the spirits of the *Sídhe* dwelling discreetly in their earthen mounds, sits comfortably enough in the context of a story-sequence in which the magical dimension never feels far away.

IT WAS THE FIRST TIME FIONN WAS EVER SEEN TO SHED A TEAR.

PART OF THE SCENERY

In Scotland, as in Ireland, ancient myth is embedded in the landscape, as it has been interpreted and absorbed into human consciousness over the centuries. Fionn mac Cumhaill is no stranger here: in some sources, indeed, driven into exile by his fear of his father's killer, Goll, he spent the greater part of his boyhood in Scotland. For as long as anyone on the Hebridean island of North Uist can remember, a group of standing stones on the hillside above Loch Langais have been known as *Pobull Fhimm* ("People of Fionn", *see photograph above*). Fionn's "fireplace" (*Sórnachean Coir Fhinn*) is to be seen at Kensaleyre, beside Loch Eyre on Skye: the two vast megaliths here are said to have been set up by Fionn and his friends to balance a spit to roast a deer on. Quite the cook, he has a cauldron too, *Suidhe Coire Fhionn*, on the Isle of Arran.

Fionn's son Oisín endures as well: there's a Loch Ossian at the northern edge of Rannoch Moor; an "Ossian's Cave" high up on the Aonach Dubh ("Black Ridge") of Bidean nam Bian, south of Glencoe. This is supposed to have been the secret den in which the "Little Deer" was born. He's said to have been buried across the country in the Sma' Glen (Small Glen) of Glenalmond, not far from Perth. His gravestone, a giant boulder, had to be moved out of the way – with the utmost difficulty – when England's General Wade passed this way with his engineers in the early eighteenth century. (The network of military roads he was building was designed to play its part in subduing a Scotland up in arms in response to a more modern but just as powerful myth – that of Jacobite destiny, the right to rule of the Stuart kings.) When the weary sappers finally managed to shift the stone, they found human remains buried beneath it: the body of Oisín, lying there since legendary times?

ABOVE: "Ossian's Cave", at the Hermitage of Dunkeld, Perth and Kinross, is a romantic "folly", dating from the eighteenth century.

Folkloric Foolery

Whether waking or sleeping, Fionn mac Cumhaill lives on in legends like these. In that respect he'll surely never die. But legends take on lives of their own – hence the differences (and, at times, the bewildering inconsistencies) between the available versions not just of Fionn's but of many other mythic stories. Just as Christian scribes (it seems likely) reproduced their own, de-paganized versions of great epics like the *Táin Bó Cúailnge*, which introduced mortal men and women – albeit great ones – in place of deities, so in later centuries, as the advent of modern science and learning pushed the old beliefs further out towards the very margins of the popular consciousness, they were reinterpreted yet again as fairytale ogres and suchlike. Their province no longer the ninth-century mead hall nor the twelfth-century monastic cloister, these figures now had the nursery, or the pub, for their stamping ground. So we find them enacting outlandish roles in children's stories or (treated with rather more sexual knowingness or satiric irreverence) in shaggy-dog stories for a more sophisticated, adult audience.

Clash of the Titans

One typical story of this type brings the two giants of Irish mythic tradition together – quite literally as giants. Fionn and Cú Chulainn are both monstrous specimens – but also semi-comic figures – here. Fionn, it is said, was at this time hard at work on the vast road he was building between Ireland and Scotland – we call the only part that now remains the Giant's Causeway. Meanwhile, the news reached Fionn that the notorious Cú Chulainn was on his way across the causeway, keen to meet him: he'd given all the giants in Scotland a beating and now it was to be Ireland's turn. Fionn, of course, was first in line: his reputation was considerable, and he was revered as the heavyweight champion of Irish giants.

HE HAD NO DOUBT OF HIS ABILITY TO FLATTEN FIONN.

But Cú Chulainn was entirely unimpressed: he carried in his pocket a pancake-like little flap he'd made of a bolt of lightning that he had squashed with a single blow of his massive fist. He had no doubt of his ability to flatten Fionn in the same way – nor, it seems, did his opponent, for Fionn was suddenly seized with a yen to go home and visit his wife Oonagh. Grabbing a nearby pine tree and stripping off the branches, he promptly made a stick and set off walking. Surprised to see him but not displeased, Oonagh immediately made him welcome, but it wasn't long before she saw that something was on his mind. When Fionn told her Cú Chulainn was coming, she didn't panic. Even so, she had no idea what to do.

Only at the very last minute, the earth shaking beneath them, the walls vibrating and the windows and crockery rattling at Cú Chulainn's approaching footfall, did the answer come to her. "You have to be your baby", she told Fionn. Pushing him towards the cot in the corner, she covered him up with bedding. He was to lie there and say nothing, she told her husband. Moments later, Cú Chulainn was at the door: Oonagh ushered him into the house and made him welcome. But when she heard he'd come to fight Fionn, she roared with laughter and spoke to him with scorn. Even now, she said, her husband was out tearing up the countryside searching for this rash whippersnapper Cú Chulainn who was said to have presumed to challenge him. Looking him up and down disdainfully, she asked her visitor if he had any idea how big and strong her husband was in comparison to a malnourished weed like him.

Cú Chulainn, a little discomfited, now took a bite from the cake Oonagh had given him: he lost two teeth against an iron bar she'd baked inside it. What was his problem? Oonagh asked. Fionn insisted on food that had a bit of bite to it, to work those

BELOW: **The Giant's Causeway, on the Antrim coast, is all that's left of Fionn mac Cumhaill's great Ireland–Scotland road.**

massive jaws of his. Their baby son was the same, she said, nodding towards the cot.

Walking over to the corner, Oonagh gave her husband another cake – this one without any iron in it: he took a bite and it broke clean in half. Cú Chulainn, bemused, walked over to see this prodigious infant for himself: if this was the baby, what must the man be like? He wanted to feel for himself the teeth that could bite a cake like that. Leaning over the cot and crooning, he pushed his finger deep into the "baby's" mouth, poking around inside to find these amazing teeth.

FIONN INSISTED ON FOOD THAT HAD A BIT OF BITE.

Chomp! Fionn snapped off the probing digit with a single bite. That Cú Chulainn was in excruciating pain was only the start of his problems now. If Fionn kept all his wisdom in his thumb, Cú Chulainn's immense strength was all stored in this finger. Without it, he was as weak as a real baby. Fionn's fears forgotten, he leapt out of the cot and set about his enemy with all his giant's strength. In no time, the great Cú Chulainn was a corpse.

4

THE MABINOGION OF WALES

Bundled together in the eighteenth century from a stock of stories first written down in the Middle Ages, the Welsh work known as the *Mabinogion* is a curious confection, yet firmly founded in Celtic myth.

The half-timbered pub is a Victorian copy – as, for that matter, is the "medieval" cross in the "village" centre (although its steps are the real deal: eight centuries old). Even so, as suburbs go Bromborough is no more brashly, boringly modern than most, and more attractive than many – it is one of Merseyside's leafiest, indeed. You'd hardly guess to look at the place that some serious history seems likely to have happened here; that this place may have been the site of a military engagement that was to decide the destinies of nations. For Bromborough, a great many scholars

OPPOSITE: Llech Ronw, northwest Wales: the hole was left by Lleu's spear, which flew clean through it to kill Gronw.

ABOVE: The chaos at Brunanburh (937) reflected the complex ethno-politics of Britain at the time.

believe, was in 937 the scene of the Battle of Brunanburh, commemorated in an important Old English poem of that name. "The field flowed with the blood of the fighters", marvelled the Anglo-Saxon bard, "from the moment the sun – God's star; the candle of the Eternal Lord – rose up to light the day and floated across above the earth until the time when it sank beneath the far horizon." The engagement brought a coalition of Celtic forces, from Scotland and Wales, together with a Norse–Gael force from Dublin (now a Viking centre) against the army of King Aethelstan of England. While it has often been identified as the moment when "England" as an entity came into being, the battle marked as pivotal a point for the Celtic countries. For Wales in particular, perhaps, this was the moment when what had been a proud history first showed signs of losing definition, of melting away, its clear narrative dissolving into myth. Its people were to rise again repeatedly – indeed they were never to surrender their national pride. As an independent nation, though, they were living on borrowed time.

Ruination

If Armagh's Fort Navan doesn't quite measure up to its epic memorialization as the Emain Macha of Ulster's King Conchobar, Caerleon falls still shorter of its ancient reputation. In Geoffrey of Monmouth's twelfth-century *History of the British Kings*, what is now a ruined Roman camp in the suburban outskirts of Newport, in South Wales, is invested with the most illustrious of pasts.

Britain's proudest, most majestic metropolis, this was the great King Arthur's capital, no less. The chronicler writes:

"Besides its great wealth above the other cities, its situation, which was in Glamorganshire upon the river Uske, near the Severn sea, was most pleasant, and fit for so great a solemnity. For on one side it was washed by that noble river, so that the kings and princes from the countries beyond the seas might have the convenience of sailing up to it. On the other side, the beauty of the meadows and groves, and magnificence of the royal palaces with lofty gilded roofs that adorned it, made it even rival the grandeur of Rome."

The comparison with Rome is provocative – and ironically appropriate. The archeological record suggests that such "magnificence" as Caerleon ever possessed had been conferred on it by the region's Roman occupiers in the centuries before King Arthur was supposed to have lived. Geoffrey knew that what he elsewhere describes as the "City of Legions" had been a Roman centre. But he wasn't prepared to forgo the idea of a more recent and romantic past. In this particular "history", following Rome's fifth-century withdrawal, the Anglo-Saxon invaders had been held back from what was now imagined as the British – and, ultimately, Celtic – land of Wales.

BELOW: Impressive as it is, the Roman amphitheatre at Caerleon can't match the magnificence the place once had in Celtic myth.

The Waltons

The Celtic inheritance of Wales is commemorated in the country's French name, *Pays de Galles* and its Spanish, *Gales*. The English "Wales" has its origins in the Anglo-Saxon word *wealas* ("foreigners"): a dark land, defined by its otherness, in short. Yet, convenient as it may have been to divide the new country into comfortable homeland and hostile alien territory, that wasn't really how things were shaping up on the ground. Celtic life and culture endured – at least for a while, and at least in little pockets – in the midst of a prevailingly proto-English Anglo-Saxon culture.

Hence the proliferation of the place-name "Walton", with its literal meaning of "Settlement of the Wealas": examples are to be found the length and breadth of England. There are well over 20 Waltons, from Buckinghamshire to Cumbria, and from Shropshire to Warwickshire and to urban Liverpool. Then there are the compounded Waltons: -on-Thames in Surrey; -on-the-Naze in Essex; -upon-Trent in Derbyshire; -on-the-Wolds in Leicestershire, for example. Preston, Lancashire, boasts a Walton-le-Dale and Somerset a Walton-in-Gordano. And, of course, when colonists set out from England they took their place names with them, founding further Waltons all the way from Canada to New Zealand.

An Enduring Presence

Again, there is a certain frustration in the failure of the Celts to leave any written record of their own behind them. What might have been a great literary patrimony has come down to us only in much later, much modified – and arguably "bastardized" – versions. That said, once we find ourselves using a word like "failure" for the cultural decisions of other peoples, applying some yardstick of our own to what they "should" or "shouldn't" do, we have to stop to consider whether we have any right to make that judgment. And, in the case of the Celts at least, to wonder whether there isn't actually something exciting about the ability of an ancient mythology to "haunt" the imaginations of later and more modern literary cultures, from that of the medieval monasteries to those of the twentieth-century "Celtic Twilight" and of the present day. If we can't be sure of having any Celtic myths in their absolutely original, "pure" form, we find them a frequent – sometimes a pervasive – presence in later European literature.

That same tolerance of open-ended, indefinite forms that we found in La Tène art; that same interest in the interpenetration of shapes, the overflowing of boundaries and the dissolution of set forms perhaps made it easier for Celtic ideas and imagery to intermingle with and inspire the creativity of other, later peoples. Hence, then, the extraordinary afterlife of a Celtic aesthetic that, by the rights of historical development and social and cultural change, "should" have been well and truly dead by the middle centuries of the first millennium.

Likewise, we see the beginnings of that long-familiar opposition of a mainstream modern culture and an alien "other" in the relationship between England and Wales – and, in some ways more intriguingly, between England and the continuing strand of Celtic life and culture within itself.

Romantic Rediscovery

CELTIC MYTHS FOUND REINVENTED FORM IN A MEDIEVAL GENRE.

What appear once to have been Celtic myths found reinvented form in one particular medieval genre that was to turn out to have great staying power in itself. In one of the most famous stories of the narrative collection that has come to be known as the *Mabinogion*, a brave young knight rides out on a quest to find his lady. The tale of Culhwch and Olwen is, very loosely, what we'd call a chivalric romance, all gallant knights, fair ladies and damsels in distress. The genre is most familiar to us now through the stories of King Arthur and his Knights of the Round Table. Indeed our hero here, Culhwch, is reputedly the great king's cousin.

KING OF THE CELTS?

King Arthur occupies an ambiguous position in the history of Celtic legend. In so far as there is any evidence at all for his existence (chiefly in the anonymous ninth-century chronicle the *Historia Brittonum* or "History of the Britons" and Geoffrey of Monmouth's twelfth-century *Historia Regum Britanniae* or "History of the British Kings"), Arthur Pendragon was a leader of British resistance against the invading Anglo-Saxons. That would make him a pretty convincing Celtic hero.

Yet the great bulk of what we "know" about Arthur, his Knights of the Round Table (like Lancelot, Gawain and Percival), his court at Camelot, his biography from boyhood to his marriage with Queen Guinevere and the story of the Quest for the Holy Grail, was the creation of high medieval writers – often "foreign" ones like the French Chrétien de Troyes or the German Wolfram von Eschenbach. They were writing out of a much later, explicitly Christian courtly tradition, with very different values from those of the ancient Celts – or even more recent works like the Irish *Táin Bó Cúailnge*. Even so, at a deeper level the Arthurian romances do partake of the imagery and themes of earlier Celtic legend. The mysterious "Green Knight" who challenges Sir Gawain, for example, may be seen as a spirit of nature as a symbol of Christ's sacrifice. Despite its obvious connection with the Last Supper of the Gospels, the Holy Grail fits easily enough into a long succession of sacred and symbolic Celtic receptacles from the Gundestrup Cauldron to Pryderi's Golden Bowl.

If the great mythic cycles of Celtic Ireland went through radical changes in the hands of monastic scribes, those that have come to us by way of the high-medieval romance tradition have surely been distorted even more. The famous French poet Chrétien de Troyes (late-twelfth century); the German author of *Tristan* Gottfried von Strassburg (late twelfth and early thirteenth centuries), and their hosts of imitators worked hard to evoke a world in which warlike deeds were no more than strands in a sophisticated tapestry to which the principles of aristocratic honour, courtesy, extravagantly expressed gallantry and love were ultimately every bit as crucial. The knight errant, heading off alone on his quest through the world, whether to secure the prize that would prove his love for his fair lady or on a more metaphorical (even metaphysical) search to find some special meaning, was to capture the imagination of subsequent generations. Although a figure of ridicule by the time of Cervantes at the start of the seventeenth century, Don Quixote left him down but not completely out and he was to resurface again in much more recent times.

WARLIKE DEEDS WERE STRANDS IN A SOPHISTICATED TAPESTRY.

BELOW: Wolfram von Eschenbach's dashing knight Parzifal (Sir Percival) sets out on his chivalric quest.

The chivalric tradition was rediscovered by a nineteenth century reacting against the economic philistinism and mechanistic mass-production of the Industrial Age. At a time that appeared, in Wilde's words, to know "the price of everything and the value of nothing", the knight's extravagant ardour – and heroic self-sacrifice – stirred the heart. As they still do, although they seem terribly remote from the sort of values celebrated

by the Celts (in so far as these can genuinely be judged from
the classical commentators or the Irish legends). Certainly, as
reinterpreted and re-romanticized in the poetry of Alfred, Lord
Tennyson, and in the paintings of the Pre-Raphaelite
Brotherhood, these stories took on a hazy aura of
wistfulness and loss that it is hard to imagine the
ancient bards being able to relate to. Even so, this
is arguably the form in which the Celtic myths
have most obviously endured into modern times.
Its reimagining in the works of J.R.R. Tolkien was
ultimately to lead to an explosion of popularity in the
"Sword and Sorcery" fictions of the present day.

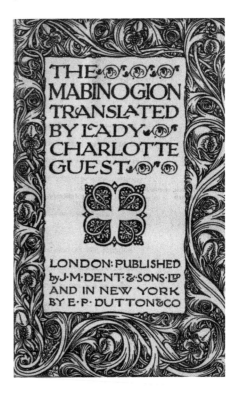

The *Mabinogion* Metamorphoses

The so-called *Mabinogion* embodies this basic
progression from ancient legend to modern fantasy.
In fact, its status as a single and coherent work would
appear to have no basis whatsoever in Celtic reality
– even though it is made up of assorted narrative
odds and ends that do. Taking its name from the
old Welsh word *mab* for "boy" or "youth", this rich
and complex collection of stories has as its ultimate
sources a wide variety of ancient myths. Long circulated in the
oral tradition, these were eventually written down in the twelfth
and thirteenth centuries by a variety of different scribes, then lost
from sight before being rediscovered in the eighteenth century.

Modernity didn't know what to make of it: its very title
was based on a misunderstanding, *Mabinogion* being the inept
pluralization of what was already a plural word in Welsh. (The
significance of the boys or youths of the title was unclear as
well: William Owen Pughe, in his 1795 translation, interpreted
Mabinogion as meaning simply "Juvenile Amusements"; other
scholars saw the collection as a study manual for "young poets".)
The work was fixed, for most modern readers, in its translation by
the aristocratic educationalist and scholar, Lady Charlotte Guest.
Her wonderfully readable translation, the result of years of work,
was finally published in 1849 and was to be an inspiration for the
whole Victorian age.

ABOVE: Not just a
translation but the
unravelling of an
impossible narrative
tangle, Lady Guest's
Mabinogion was a
historically important
work.

ABOVE: Culhwch – no fearsome warrior but a gentle, courtly knight. The nineteenth century found a new way of reading Celtic myth.

Courtly Qualities

It certainly set the tone. Perhaps the oldest narrative in the collection, Culhwch and Olwen's story as retold by Lady Guest, is nevertheless typical in picking up the grace and glamour with which the medieval romance writer invests a much more ancient plot. Rough and ready by the standards of later Arthurian romances – with little to say of life at court or the codification of chivalric values – it still shows an ideal of aristocratic nobility taking form. A gutsy narrative of heroic challenge, stoic ordeal and final triumph has here become a love story in which, while courage in combat is obviously important, courteous gentility prevails against brute monstrosity and Christian virtue carries the day over magic strength.

"And the youth pricked forth upon a steed with head dappled grey, of four winters old, firm of limb, with shell-formed hoofs, having a bridle of linked gold on his head, and upon him a saddle of costly gold." The quality of the hero's horse, and the richness of its accoutrements, matter as much as his own warlike stature, it would seem. His very weaponry is described with a loving, consumer-conscious care that, while acknowledging epic conventions ("an edge to wound the wind") in passing, recalls the modern "sex and shopping" novel more readily than it does the *Táin Bó Cúailnge*:

"And in the youth's hand were two spears of silver, sharp, well-tempered, headed with steel, three ells in length, of an edge to wound the wind, and cause blood to flow, and swifter than the fall of the dewdrop from the blade of reed-grass upon the earth when the dew of June is at the heaviest. A gold-hilted sword was upon his thigh, the blade of which was of gold, bearing a cross of inlaid gold of the hue of the lightning of heaven: his war-horn was of ivory. Before him were two brindled white-breasted greyhounds, having strong collars of rubies about their necks, reaching from the shoulder to the ear. And the one that was on the left side bounded across to the right side, and the one on the right to the left, and like two sea-swallows sported around him. And his courser cast up four sods with his four hoofs, like four swallows in the air, about his head, now above, now below."

We're even told the value of important items of knightly costume – although, with quaint archaism, this is measured in number of cattle ("kine").

"About him was a four-cornered cloth of purple, and an apple of gold was at each corner, and every one of the apples was of the value of an hundred kine. And there was precious gold of the value of three hundred kine upon his shoes, and upon his stirrups, from his knee to the tip of his toe."

BELOW: **A wooden wizard's head: one of many Mabinogion figures found represented in Cwmcarn Forest, north of Newport in South Wales.**

Altogether, then, a majestic sight, and yet somehow at the same time an insubstantial one: as a physical presence, this hero is hardly there at all. We've come a long way from the "wild beasts" the Romans feared. There's little danger of our confusing this young knight errant with Cú Chulainn or with Fionn. (Even before their later reinvention as comic giants.) So exquisite is Culhwch's grace, he seems to float along:

"And the blade of grass bent not beneath him, so light was his courser's tread as he journeyed towards the gate of Arthur's Palace."

But if he isn't the hulking hero of the past, this gentle knight is nevertheless completely Celtic in his closeness to nature, in the harmony that exists between him, his horse and the environment in which it moves.

Family Drama

Not that this wider cosmic order extends down into the domestic sphere from which Culhwch may be seen to be escaping. The young prince, we're told, was the son of King Cilydd, borne to him by Goleuddydd, his beloved

Maker of the Mabinogion

Born in the thoroughly un-Celtic county of Lincolnshire, eastern England, in 1812, Lady Charlotte Bertie (*below*) was the daughter of the Earl of Lindsey. At a time when the aristocratic young lady's life kept her in the narrowest of spheres – however exalted – she was very soon trying hard to extend her horizons. While some facility in French and Italian was valued as a ladylike

"accomplishment", young Charlotte went far beyond what was usual – or even seemly. She tackled Greek and Latin too, before going on – essentially unassisted – to master Hebrew, Arabic and Persian.

At the age of 21 she married Josiah Guest, an MP and a wealthy manufacturer with an ironworks at Dowlais, near Merthyr Tydfil in South Wales. There she took an active role in organizing workers' education. She also continued her own, taking the opportunity to familiarize herself with the language and the literature of her new home country. In between her philanthropic projects she took an increasing role as assistant manager to her now ailing husband in his ironworks.

In keeping with a nineteenth-century view of the Celts as romantic rebels, the translator of the *Mabinogion* was a wayward spirit and a defier of convention. The forgotten literary traditions of a disdained and disparaged Wales were not the only unworthy cause she espoused in the eyes of her own class. Despite his distinction and wealth, Josiah was "below" Lady Charlotte in social rank, and this had raised eyebrows when the two were wed. When, after his death in 1852, Charlotte married Charles Schreiber, a classical scholar – and her son's sometime tutor – she found herself systematically shunned, and spent the next years travelling with him in Europe.

Queen. During her pregnancy, however, she had gone mad, taking to the fields and mountains, wandering without direction, living like a beast in the wilderness. Finally one night, finding shelter in a dilapidated, low-roofed structure in a field, she was startled by the sudden appearance of the great sow whose home this actually was. So shocked was Goleuddydd that she went into convulsions and gave birth right there and then, so Cilydd's crown prince was brought to light in the mud and stench of a tumbledown pigsty. The trauma killed her, leaving the infant Culhwch orphaned at the very start of his existence.

When a peasant found the queen lying helpless and dying beside her child, amid the mud and the manure, he promptly told King Cilydd, who had her brought back to him at his royal palace with their infant son. With her last breath, she begged him not to take another wife until he found a briar above her grave boasting two blossoms, to show that her soul was at last at rest. Cilydd gave her his word, and promised too that he would look after their son with devotion. He called him Culhwch, and he was brought up – very happily – at the court. Every year thereafter, the king went regularly to his late wife's grave, which he had his servants keep clear of weeds: one year he found a briar in blossom springing from the soil. However, his counsellors told him that the only woman who was worthy of him was already married to neighbouring King Doged. No matter: Cilydd went to war and claimed "his" bride – who, thanks to the hostilities he himself had launched, was now a widow.

Not the most edifying start for a marriage, then, but one appropriate to the nature of the bride he'd chosen. The new queen was beautiful but evil, softly spoken but cunning and malevolent: literally charming, she was a lovely-seeming witch. Wishing to tie her lineage more closely in with that of her new husband, Culhwch's stepmother pressed for the prince to be married to her own daughter. She was utterly enraged when he refused.

Charm and Harm

Much too sly to show this, though, the new queen cast a spell on the young man – although she took care to dress her curse up as a generous blessing. For Culhwch, she announced with an air of beneficence, was to wed no one but Olwen, outstanding in her fame as the fairest maiden in all of Wales. The catch wasn't long in becoming clear: Olwen was the daughter of Ysbaddaden, the Giant King. So huge and hideous was Ysbaddaden that he towered over any

HIS WARTS WERE LIKE MOUNTAINS; HIS WRINKLES DEEP AS DITCHES.

human church; his very warts were like mountains; his ugly wrinkles as deep as ditches. So heavy were the folds of skin across his face that he had to prop his eyelids open with a pair of forks. And if he was a giant in physical stature, he was still more enormous in ill will.

Cilydd was concerned at his wife's announcement. He knew how dangerous Ysbaddaden was and how hard Olwen would be

BELOW: Arriving at Camelot, Culhwch was to begin with told by Arthur's porter he could not come in.

to win – although he was still too innocent to see the malice underlying his new Queen's prophecy. He did his best to discourage his son, but Culhwch found that once the thought of the giant's daughter had been planted in his mind he really couldn't get it out again over the days, weeks and months that followed. Olwen was his ideal (quite literally, in that he had of course never seen her), the yardstick by which he had come to measure all feminine beauty and virtue – and against which all other maidens fell so badly short. The summation of all he sought in life, she was the embodiment of all he wanted; she was his goal, his aim, the star he had to follow. Winning her, he resolved, was both his destiny and his duty.

Faced with this reality, Culhwch's father reluctantly set aside his resistance and bestowed his blessing on his son's great quest. He knew, however, that the young knight would never be able to win his heart's desire without the backing of King Arthur, Cilydd's nephew, and Culhwch's cousin. Hence, then, the scene we saw before, with the young Welsh prince "pricking" – spurring on his "steed", or "courser" – his elegant, weightless way across an open landscape, the country before him an endless arena of adventure, his first stop the gates of Camelot and Arthur's court.

Kilwch arrives at the Gate of Arthur's Palace

A Liminal Legend

Foundling children are the standard stuff of fairytale, of course, and don't necessarily raise an eyebrow in the reader, but the circumstances in which Culhwch's story starts are still disturbing. The violence of his mother's madness; the traumatic abruptness of his own birth in the pigsty – and the strength of the animal associations that confers on him; the sinister threat of a quasi-incestuous marriage with a step-sister; the casting of a

OPPOSITE: Pigs were prestigious in Celtic tradition: this (apparently quite cuddly) boar is to be found in Cwmcarn Forest.

PORCINE PRESTIGE

There is an unmistakable dissonance for us today between certain symbolic elements in Culhwch's story and the romantic, chivalrous narrative that now contain them. The very name "Culhwch" seems incongruous to us – once, at least, we've understood that it means something like "Little Pig". It may be an appropriate enough handle for one of the Welsh prince's place of birth, but it hardly helps confer courtly status on this noble knight.

Seen in a longer historical perspective and a wider Celtic context, though, it is less insulting than we might assume. The Celts were a farming people, and their pigs prized for their meat and hide. Omnivorous calorific converters, pigs could eat just about anything and turn it into fertilizing dung; like living ploughs, they broke up the ground as they snuffled after food.

Plumpness didn't seem unappealing to a people struggling constantly to keep starvation at bay. What could be more pleasing than the plenty it seemed to signify? Hence the symbolism that set a mighty sow atop the hillock-home of the Irish Daghda, as improbable an image of divinity as this may seem to us today. Earlier myths assert that the first pigs were given to Prince Pryderi of Dyfed, mid-Wales, by King Arawn of the Underworld. Successive lords of Gwynedd, Dyfed's northern neighbour, attempted to take what were already regarded as totemic animals in a series of wars every bit as fierce as those fought in Ireland over the bulls of Ulster and of Connacht.

curse by an unnatural mother-monster … Culhwch's story draws on dark and elemental fears of a type that seem to take us back, far beyond the dreamy romanticism of the Arthurian legend to the very beginnings of a Celtic – even a human – consciousness. Reinterpreted by the medieval romance writer as a chivalric *geste* or adventure, though, it takes on elegant aspects of grace and gallantry.

A Curse and a Blessing

Still, though, there is that deeper, darker side. Culhwch was quickly thwarted in his purpose, finding his way into Arthur's palace firmly barred by the porter, Glewlwyd. The king was feasting, he said, and could not be interrupted. Culhwch threatened a curse that touched on profound primeval fears. If he didn't open up, the young knight swore,

"I will bring disgrace upon thy Lord, and evil report upon thee. And I will set up three shouts at this very gate, than which none were ever more deadly, from the top of Pengwaed in Cornwall to the bottom of Dinsol, in the North, and to

Esgair Oervel, in Ireland. And all the women in this Palace that are pregnant shall lose their offspring; and such as are not pregnant, their hearts shall be turned by illness, so that they shall never bear children from this day forward."

Moved by a menace that went to the very heart of life at Arthur's court, the porter reported to his king and told him of his visitor – how handsome he was, and what dignity he possessed. Despite his advisors' cautions that he should not break with generations of convention, Arthur bade him bring the man to join him as their new guest. When he saw

HOW HANDSOME HE WAS, AND WHAT DIGNITY HE POSSESSED.

Culhwch walk into his hall, he was glad he had. Bidding the youth sit down, he was surprised to find his offer of hospitality refused. The prince wished to have the promise of his support, he said, but would then be on his way. When King Arthur offered him anything he wanted, Culhwch replied merely that he wanted the king to bless his hair. Arthur agreed, and took out a comb of gold to groom his guest.

BELOW: King Arthur holds court in Camelot, as represented in a manuscript from fourteenth-century France.

As he teased out the tangles, he felt the warmth of kinship emanating from the young man's head. He asked him who he was, and his feelings were confirmed: "I am your cousin". After the prince had told his story, King Arthur said, "Ask me anything you want, and I will help." All he wanted, Culhwch replied, was his help – and that of his knights – in winning Olwen, celebrated as the loveliest maiden in all of Wales. Famous she might be, but the king had no idea where he might find her. He sent out messengers to seek her across his realms and far beyond. A year later, though, they'd all returned and not one had found so much as a trace of a girl who it seemed was as retiring as she was renowned. So illustrious was her reputation that it had actually effaced her physical reality: this fair paragon was nowhere to be found.

The Magnificent Seven

It was time to get serious, King Arthur decided. He sent six of his best knights out with Culhwch to help him in his quest. Cai was naturally his first choice: this man could make himself a giant at will, manage nine days and nights without the need for sleep and nine days and nights under water without needing air. His body had such natural heat that it kept him dry in the heaviest rainstorm, while in the coldest weather his hands could light a fire. As for his warlike prowess, his sword made wounds that simply would not heal. He was an indispensable helper on any battlefield. With him went Bedwyr, his friend, the fastest runner in the whole of Britain and the quickest with his weapons – his lance

BELOW: Arthur's round table was traditionally assumed to do away with hierarchy and promote true brotherhood among his knights.

could do the work of nine. Then there was Cynddelig, who could find his way through the strangest territory as though it were his own, and Gwrhyr Gwalstawd Ieithoedd, who spoke every language known to man. With them went the enchanted Menw, who could change his shape at will, as well as Gewalchmai, the "best of knights" – and Arthur's nephew.

Off they went into the wide world, travelling for many days over high hills and through deep and barely penetrable forests, before, finally, they found themselves emerging on to an open grassy plain. Beneath a vast and vaulting sky they looked across to the far horizon where they saw a great castle rising upward from the ground. With hopes rising in their hearts, they set their spurs to their horses' sides and started off at a brisk trot; by nightfall, they thought, they would have a comfortable bed. Evening came, however, and the castle was as far away as ever – that meant another night on the cold ground. All next day they journeyed on. By nightfall, though, the castle seemed every bit as far removed and they had to settle down once again in the open air. The third day they fared no better; not until the fourth sunset was approaching did they see the castle looming up before them, at last in reach.

A Brother Brought Low

But their way was barred by the biggest flock of sheep that any of them had ever encountered. It stretched as far as the eye could see to either side. Looking around for their shepherd, Culhwch and his companions saw him sitting on a nearby hill while he watched over his sheep. They approached and asked him whose sheep he tended, and to whom the castle in the background belonged: the answer to both questions, he said sorrowfully, was Ysbaddaden. Inviting the strangers to join him for a meal in his cottage, he introduced himself as Custennin, the brother Ysbaddaden had cruelly dispossessed to take his birthright. Taking them inside, he introduced his wife – once it was apparent that the coast was clear, a young man emerged from his hiding place inside a big stone chest in a corner of the room. Of all their 24 sons, he was the only one the giant had left alive. So bleak had the boy's prospects always seemed that they hadn't wanted to tempt fate even by giving him a name. To this day, then, he was as anonymous – and as shy and timid – as a wild creature. This was no way to live, the knights agreed. Cai asked Custennin if he could free the boy from his life of hiding and take

THEY FOUND THEMSELVES EMERGING ON TO AN OPEN, GRASSY PLAIN.

LEFT: "The maiden was clothed in flame-coloured silk." Culhwch has his first sight of Olwen – and promptly falls in love.

him with him; he would look after him, make him his squire and, ultimately, a knight.

Hearing that Culhwch had come to win the hand of Olwen, the woman of the house confessed that she had mixed feelings: she rejoiced for the girl – whom everybody loved – but was bitterly sad for her would-be suitor. Others had gone to seek her hand, but none had ever returned. A maiden Ysbaddaden's daughter still remained. The giant wasn't just a jealous father: as long as his daughter was unwed, he would remain immortal, but if she should ever marry he would die. That would be no loss to the world, though, Custennin's wife acknowledged: as long as they would promise to do the giant's daughter no harm, she would send for Olwen so the young man might at the very least meet her. But she begged him to reconsider, and to return whence he had come: no girl was beautiful enough to run the risk of dying for – and in this case death was pretty much a certainty. Culhwch was determined, though – and even more so once the young lady had arrived.

A NATURAL BEAUTY

No literary genre is more unabashedly artificial than the chivalric romance of the Middle Ages, and Olwen's appearance is described every bit as extravagantly as might be expected. "The maiden was clothed in a robe of flame-coloured silk", we are told in Lady Guest's translation: "and about her neck was a collar of ruddy gold, on which were precious emeralds and rubies." So sumptuous a tone is set in the description of these accessories that it's easy to miss the subtle shift when the narrator gets on to Olwen's actual person – for which comparisons are drawn direct from nature:

> "More yellow was her head than the flower of the broom, and her skin was whiter than the foam of the wave, and fairer were her hands and her fingers than the blossoms of the wood anemone amidst the spray of the meadow fountain. The eye of the trained hawk, the glance of the three-mewed falcon was not brighter than hers. Her bosom was more snowy than the breast of the white swan, her cheek was redder than the reddest roses. Whoso beheld her was filled with her love."

It is no more than a memory, an ancient instinct reduced to the status of a literary flourish, but this description nevertheless recalls the human-animal hybrids – and, more generally, the boundary-breaking aesthetic – of the La Tène era. The name "Olwen" in medieval Welsh literally meant "white footprint", we're told. And, indeed, we're assured that "Four white trefoils sprung up wherever she trod".

A Fateful Meeting

As celebrated as Olwen's beauty was, the descriptions fell far short: Culhwch flung himself down before her and begged her for her hand. Olwen shook her head sadly. She was a dutiful daughter, she said, and had given her word not to attach herself without her father's sanction. She felt real warmth towards him: that was clear. She would help the prince in whatever way she could. First, though, they'd have to gain access to the castle; then, she said, there'd be Ysbaddaden to confront: she insisted that Culhwch should agree to anything her father asked of him, however alarming.

An Unfriendly Father

Olwen bade them follow, and they set out with her in wary silence. Circling the castle, they stopped at its nine gates in turn. At each, they quietly killed the guard and dispatched the watchdog with him before it could so much as growl. The castle laid wide open to them now, they walked in with Olwen and found themselves in the presence of a startled Ysbaddaden. "We're here to ask for your daughter's hand, for Prince Culhwch, son of Cilydd", they announced.

"Where," he asked, "are my gatekeepers? My servants? Lift up the forks upon my eyes so I may look on my son-in-law." They obliged, and he surprised them then by the calm of his response. "Go now," he said. "But come back tomorrow, and you'll have your reply." As they left his hall, however, he picked up a poison dart from the floor beside his chair and sent it scudding after them across the room. But Bedwyr, quick as always, heard it hiss through the air behind them and turned and snatched it. Before anyone else could even react, he'd sent it shooting back at Ysbaddaden. It caught him at the knee and made him double up with pain.

Back to Custennin's home they went: when they returned to see Ysbaddaden the next day they found him once again composed and calm. Again, though, he sent them off to await

BELOW: **Rhiannon reputedly first appeared to Pryderi on this mound – now Narbeth Castle, Pembrokeshire.**

ABOVE: Culhwch confronts Ysbaddaden outside his castle. The giant was ready to fight, as the picture shows.

his reply – and again as they left he flung a dart after them. Fortunately, Menw sensed its presence, caught it and threw it back. This one went right through the giant's thorax and came out the other side. Even so, he was poised and courteous when the next day Prince Culhwch and the knights arrived to see him for the third time. This time, Ysbaddaden grabbed his dart while his visitors were actually addressing him. He hurled it at Culhwch, but the young man caught it and threw it right back. It hit the Giant King in the eye, and went right through to penetrate his head – and, again, it came out the other side. Ysbaddaden writhed in agony: once more, though, he quickly collected himself, asking his visitors to come back and see him the next day. Then, he assured them, they really would get their answer.

A Few Favours…

They duly arrived and, having first warned Ysbaddaden not to attack them again, Culhwch asked him for his daughter's hand.

"Sure," he said, "just so long as you grant me a few favours I will ask you."

"Granted," the delighted Culhwch replied. "What are they?"

"Well," said the King of Giants: "Seest thou yonder vast hill? … I require that it be rooted up, and that the grubbings be burned for manure on the face of the land, and that it be ploughed and sown in one day, and in one day that the grain ripen. And of that wheat I intend to make food and liquor fit for the wedding of thee and my daughter. And all this I require done in one day."

If Culhwch felt disconcerted, he was certainly not going to let that show: "It will be easy for me to compass this, although thou mayest think that it will not be easy", he replied.

The giant wasn't done: "Though this be easy for thee", he said, "there is yet that which will not be so. No husbandman can till or prepare this land, so wild is it, except Amaethon the son of Don, and he will not come with thee by his own free will, and thou wilt not be able to compel him."

"It will be easy for me to compass this, although thou mayest think that it will not be easy."

"Though thou get this, there is yet that which thou wilt not get. Govannon the son of Don to come to the headland to rid the iron, he will do no work of his own good will except for a lawful king, and thou wilt not be able to compel him."

"It will be easy for me to compass this."

"Though thou get this, there is yet that which thou wilt not get; the two dun oxen of Gwlwlyd, both yoked together, to plough the wild land yonder stoutly. He will not give them of his own free will, and thou wilt not be able to compel him."

Ysbaddaden was barely getting into his stride: the demands kept coming, thick and fast – pure honey, nine times sweeter than that usually made by bees, came next, for making mead. Then it was a special drinking cup, the property of Llwyr, son of Llwyryon, which would hold endless amounts of drink without ever running dry; then there was a magic basket that was always and infinitely full of whatever anybody wished to find inside. To make his banquet go with even more of a swing, Ysbaddaden wanted Teirtu's enchanted harp – it played itself, the most moving, the most stirring and the sweetest songs. The

THE DEMANDS KEPT COMING, THICK AND FAST, EACH ONE INDISPENSABLE.

list went on and on, and every single item was, the giant said, an indispensable demand: if Culhwch failed him, he could forget marrying his daughter. Of all these things, though, he particularly wanted the prince to get hold of Drudwyn, the dog of Greid, the son of Eri. It might have gone without saying (but of course it didn't: so long and comprehensive was Ysbaddaden's screed) that

ABOVE: **Dying of grief at the war fought over her in Ireland, Branwen died and was buried here at Llanddeusant, Anglesey.**

this extraordinary hound could only possibly be tethered with a special lead (made with hair from the beard of Dillus Varvawc, an infamous robber-giant) – and that this in its turn had to be attached to a certain special collar guarded jealously by the hundred-handed monster, Canhastyr Canllaw.

There were – inevitably – several further twists: Drudwyn could only be captured by the benign enchantments of one man, Mabon ap Modron. Like Olwen herself, he was a figure of whose significance everybody was aware but whose whereabouts nobody seemed to know. He had been abducted from his mother by an unknown enemy when he was only three days old, and had reputedly been held prisoner in some unknown location ever since. Drudwyn had to be secured, because he was the only hound who was capable of hunting the prize Ysbaddaden most desperately wanted – the great wild boar, the Twrch Twyth. This giant, ferocious animal had once been a king of Ireland: he owed his present guise to a curse – and he was filled with fury at his plight. Between his ears, however, were held a special comb and scissors – the only ones strong enough to find their way through Ysbaddaden's thick and tangled hair. Both had to be torn directly from the head of the living, raging boar – if they weren't, they'd lose all their strength and be no use.

HE'D BE BACK IN NO TIME TO CLAIM HIS BRIDE.

Inwardly, Culhwch may have despaired, but he kept his head high and showed nothing but the most confident aplomb. Thanking his host, he said his fond goodbyes as his soon-to-be son-in-law. He'd be back in no time, he assured him, to claim his bride.

Animal Advisors

Back at Camelot, King Arthur asked Culhwch and his companions how they had fared. When he heard what Ysbaddaden was demanding, Arthur called up all his knights, his foot soldiers and his fleet: no expense or effort was going to be spared if it would help his cousin. In the meantime, though, the first priority appeared to be to find Mabon ap Modron, because he seemed to be the key to so much else. Cai and Bedwyr went in search of him: finding neither hide nor hair, they asked the animals. First, they approached the Ousel (a thrush-like bird) of Cilgwri, not

BELOW: **The Owl of Cwm Cowlyd, among the wisest creatures in the world, lived in the woods around Llyn Cowlyd, Snowdonia.**

SALMON AND SON

Mabon ap Modron translates in modern English as "Mabon, son of Modron", as though the name simply reflected an ancient patriarchal norm. But, as its resemblance to the modern word "matron" suggests, Modron seems once to have been a goddess – like, for example, the Irish Anu. Or, for that matter, the Romano-Gaulish *Dea Matrona*, who is believed to have given her name to France's River Marne. As for "Mabon", in early Welsh that word seems simply to have meant "son".

Mabon ap Modron's presence accordingly carries us back to the story's Celtic roots, just as the Salmon of Llyn Llyw takes the two heroes to their goal. As for us, that aged fish ferries us back to ancient Irish myths, like that of the Salmon of Wisdom, whose flesh was first tasted by Fionn mac Cumhaill. The other animals here in their different ways hint at a deeper symbolic resonance we can't necessarily comprehend, although it's easy enough to associate the stag with masculinity, speed and strength; the eagle with both soaring grace and regal grandeur. As for the ousel: birds in general seem to have been (literally) looked up to by the Celts, simply because their ability to fly was felt to make them intermediaries between earth and heaven.

The way in which each of the animals passes the heroes on to its elder, in an ascending scale of seniority, in this story makes of Mabon – the original man – the oldest being on earth. (Except of course, in that being at the same time – as his name suggests – the quintessential "son", his very existence suggests an older chronology and an eternal round of birth and death.) His narrative of abduction immediately after birth, of subsequent imprisonment and final release – a symbolic rebirth – can be interpreted equally convincingly as representing a Christian redemption or a pagan continuity of lives.

far from Corwen. He couldn't help, he said: he lacked the age and wisdom; he advised them to find his elder brother, the Stag of Rhedynfre, who in turn sent them to the – even older – Owl of Cwm Cowlyd (in Snowdonia's Carneddau Mountains). Old and wise as he was, this bird admitted he was not as venerable or knowledgeable as the Eagle of Gwernabwy. Reluctant as that raptor was to confess it, he was not the oldest animal, or the wisest, he said: he directed Cai and Bedwyr to the shores of Llyn Llyw – "The Lake of the Leader". Here a salmon, the oldest living creature in the world, was to be found: he could be relied upon to know everything that could be known. And so it proved: the great fish took them on its back and bore them away downriver all the way to Gloucester, from the dungeons of whose castle they could faintly hear a captive's cries.

The king arrived from Camelot with reinforcements and attacked the castle from the fore, while the salmon carried Cai and Bedwyr back around the rear by river. Standing on his shoulders, while the garrison was occupied with Arthur's men they were able to chip away at the stonewall and make their entrance. They found Mabon alone and weeping in his cell. Overjoyed as he was to be gaining his liberty at long last, there was no time for lengthy greetings or thanks: his rescuers whisked him off to help them in their hunt.

Boar at Bay

Before the dog Dudwyn could be captured, the special leash and collar had to be secured: each of these steps was a wild adventure in itself. While Mabon made sure of the magic hound, Arthur and his knights set off across England, Ireland, Scotland, Wales – and even France – to seek the strongest and fittest dogs to help them in their chase. Finally, the hunt was up – and an epic, even cataclysmic contest it was to prove: in his first day's flight, the Twrch Twyth laid waste a fifth of Ireland. King Arthur's men cornering him at last, scores were felled by his headlong charge and by the savage swishing of his tusks, but on the boar itself not a single mark was made.

ABOVE: Culhwch presents an astounded Ysbaddaden with the treasures he's collected – now he can collect the giant's daughter as his bride.

On the morning of the third day, King Arthur cornered the Twrch Twyth alone: through the next nine days and nights, the two thrust, parried and feinted with sword and tusk before the boar broke free and leapt across the sea to Wales. There he was brought to bay again on Cwm Kerwyn in the Preselly Mountains. More men died, although by this time the boar had sustained some wounds. Off he went again, and after a series of stands across the length and breadth of Wales he crossed the Bristol Channel into Cornwall. Mabon and Drudwyn caught up with the Twrch Twyth there, and although even now the boar could not be killed, King Arthur succeeded in snatching the comb and scissors from his head just moments before he managed to slip away and make his escape into the Atlantic Ocean.

Close Cut

Back to Ysbaddaden they went with their hard-won trophies.
Now they could give the Giant King's hair the attention it so
badly needed. After Arthur's knights had combed out the tangles
they could, hacked away those they couldn't and generally tamed
the wildness of his mane, Custennin's son stepped up, a gleaming
razor at the ready. "Now for your shave!" he said, and with a

RIGHT: "Fair Olwen":
Culhwch can barely
believe the beauty of the
woman he has won.

single stroke he swept across Ysbaddaden's throat from ear to ear, clearing away his bristles – and his skin, and the greater part of the flesh beneath. As the giant slumped, life bleeding away, Arthur and his men crowded around the youth to acclaim his deed. And to give him his name, for it finally seemed safe to end the young man's anonymity: from now on he was to be known as Goreu ("the best"). It seemed safe as well, at long, long last, for Culhwch and Olwen to be united: they were married amid general rejoicing that very evening.

The Case of the Disappearing Prince

Like the swirling shapes on a La Tène plate or shield, we see the same patterns repeating themselves in the stories of the *Mabinogion*, anticipating and echoing each other in an endless sequence. Hence we sense (although we may only actually see it when we think about it) how the tale of Goreu, kept (nameless) in a stone chest throughout his early life for fear of Ysbaddaden, parallels that of Mabon ap Modron, abducted as an infant and imprisoned. Both in turn echo the fate of another great Welsh hero, Prince Pryderi of Dyfed.

Once, the *Mabinogion* tells us, much of mid-Wales was ruled by a prince named Pwyll. One day while out hunting with his hounds, he found a fallen stag being eaten by another pack of hounds belonging to some other hunter. As prince, he saw no reason to defer to any man so he drove the dogs away

HE SAW NO REASON TO DEFER TO ANY MAN.

and allowed his own to feast on the carcase where it lay. But the hounds hadn't been just anyone's – indeed, they hadn't belonged to a man at all but to Arawn, one of the lords of Annwn, the Otherworld – that strange, ungraspable dimension occupied in Ireland by the *Sídhe*. Found out and confronted by an enraged Arawn, Pwyll apologized profusely and felt he had no alternative but to agree to whatever conditions the fairy ruler might impose. So it was that he found himself taking the other's place in his kingdom below the ground while Arawn enjoyed a year in the real world. Pwyll had to reign in Arawn's place but promised to leave his wife unmolested – an undertaking to which he

ABOVE: Appearing atop a grassy mound, with her horse of dazzling silver-grey, Rhiannon's radiance struck everyone with awe.

scrupulously adhered. It all went well: indeed, just before it was time for him to re-emerge into the light above, Pwyll fought and killed Arawn's great rival, Hafgan. Accordingly, he was able to hand over the realm of Annwn in its entirety, leaving Arawn a friend and forever in his debt. In return for his service, Arawn even gave him an honorary title: *Pwyll Pen Annwfn*, or "Pwyll, Lord of the Otherworld".

It was from this fairy kingdom, in fact, that Pwyll was to take his wife. The beautiful Rhiannon appeared before him one day in a dazzling starburst of white light, riding on a horse atop a little hill or mound (Gorsedd Arberth, near Narberth, Pembrokeshire, in southwest Wales) while he was hunting. As fast as he and his men gave chase, her horse withdrew and, however hard they rode, they could not catch her – although her own mount seemed only to be ambling along. Despairing, Pwyll called after her, whereupon she promptly halted. She wanted him, she said, rather than the prince she had been promised to. Together, they found a way of outwitting her guardians and the man her father wanted to force her into marrying, Gwawl ap Clud.

They married and became Prince and Princess of Dyfed. Their wedded bliss was complete when Rhiannon bore Pwyll a fine and handsome son – but their the happy-ever-after was rudely curtailed. The very next night, the infant was snatched away by unknown hands, and Rhiannon's ladies – fearing they would be held responsible for this most momentous of mishaps – smeared their sleeping mistress' hands and face with dog's blood to cast the blame on her. She had, they insisted the next morning, killed and eaten her own son – an act more evil than anyone could easily imagine. So Dyfed's beloved queen, now an outcast, hated and despised, Rhiannon had to do penance – sitting outside her castle and telling passers-by about her crime.

Foal Play

Meanwhile, in Gwent in the far southeast of Wales, Teyrnon Twyrf Lliant, a local lord, was exasperated: his favourite mare bore a foal each year on the eve of May Day, but every year it disappeared. When the date next came around and the animal duly gave birth, Teyrnon decided to stand watch outside her stall, and he saw a strange, clawed arm come reaching in through the stable wall. This time, before it could take the newborn animal he swung his sword and severed the arm: outside, where presumably, the monster's body had been, he found a squalling bundle. He had the baby brought inside and took it into his own household: he and his wife resolved to rear him as their own. As soon as he was old enough to walk and talk, the young boy showed a deep affinity for horses; he also showed an ever-closer resemblance to Prince Pwyll of Dyfed. Hearing the story of Pwyll and Rhiannon's stolen child, Teyrnon reluctantly realized that he and his wife had to give up their "son", for Dyfed's rulers evidently had a prior claim. Overjoyed, Pwyll and Rhiannon named their (now-grown) son Pryderi.

ABOVE: The clawed hand reaches in through the palace wall to take the infant Prince Pryderi from his crib.

Pride of Dyfed

As his father's successor, Pryderi was to become one of Wales' greatest mythic heroes. He married Cigfa, the daughter of a minor lord, but left her soon after to go to Ireland along with King Bendigeidfran (the "Blessed Crow-King"), whose daughter Branwen was being ill-used by her husband, King Matholwch. Many other British kings – outraged by these abuses – joined the invasion force. Outwitted by the treachery of Matholwch's men, the invaders were badly defeated: all but seven were cut down. (And the distraught Branwen died of a broken heart.) Pryderi was one of the survivors, though, and he brought back another, the magician-king Manawydan, who he thought would make a suitable husband for his widowed mother. (Also a survivor – after his own fashion – was Bendigeidfran himself who, although badly wounded, asked them to cut off his head and take it home to Wales with them. The head went on living, speaking and reigning over the northwest principality of Gwynedd from Bendigeidfran's throne in Harlech for a further seven years.)

HORSEPOWER

For the Celts, as for us, the horse was a powerful symbol of speed, strength and sheer beauty, but it also would have represented wealth. While racing is still the "Sport of Kings" and riding still to some extent associated with the relatively affluent, horses aren't the currency they would have been in ancient times. Hence the importance in Celtic Gaul of the horse-goddess Epona and her association not just with physical grace and prowess but with prosperity. That association "spoke" to other ancient cultures too: as open as they were to the creation of syncretic cults, the Romans didn't normally feel comfortable with the attribution of divinity to animal figures, but they made a partial exception in Epona's case. Although they gave the goddess human female form, they invariably showed her with her horse as the inseparable basis of her power. Seen this way on Roman coins and vases, Epona appears rather as Rhiannon must have done when Pwyll first saw her mounted on *her* horse; her son would also have an affinity for horses.

RIGHT: **Epona is customarily shown sitting sidesaddle on her mare.**

Manawydan and Rhiannon duly married, and the match was as successful as Pryderi had hoped. One day, however, he and Cigfa went out walking with them in the country. They found themselves passing Gorsedd Arberth – the mound upon which Pwyll had first seen Rhiannon. Walking up to the top, for old times' sake, they realized their rashness when they looked down suddenly to see the country lying ruined around them as far as the eye could see. (Like Oisín, setting his foot on the ground on his return to Ireland, they'd somehow fallen foul of the spell by which Rhiannon had first "crossed over" to this life.) They themselves were safe, but they now inhabited a completely empty wilderness, masters of a Wales that hardly existed any more.

Life went on, though, after a drab and dreary fashion, and the four kept on as best they could. One morning, the two men even went out hunting. Catching sight of a white boar, they gave pursuit and, watching as it went into the ruins of an enormous fort, they froze for a moment, uncertain as to what they should do

ABOVE: **A statue of Bendigeidfran shows the "Blessed Crow-King" outside his reputed home at Harlech Castle.**

next. Manawydan warned his son-in-law not to advance another step, but the headstrong hero wouldn't heed him and followed his quarry in. There, in an empty hall, Pryderi saw a shining bowl of gold: ignoring Manawydan's horrified cries from outside, he reached in and touched it, and was frozen to the ground. Rhiannon arrived soon after, searching for her men. She told her husband off for abandoning her son: despite his warnings, she went into the fort herself. She too put her hand into the bowl, and she too in turn was paralyzed. The fort – and the mother and son within it – melted into mist.

Left helplessly outside, Manawydan watched in stunned disbelief, but he was a potent magician in his own right. Soon

OPPOSITE: Out hunting with their dogs, Pryderi and Manawydan corner a wild white boar by a great castle.

LEFT: Pryderi was finally overcome by the sorceror-soldier Gwydion, who used an enchanted axe.

ABOVE: This stone at Maentwrog, Gwynedd, was supposedly placed to mark Pryderi's grave after the enchanter Gwydion killed him near here.

he had divined the origins of the spell that had stripped Wales first of its people and now of its prince and his mother: this was the work of the wicked sorceror Llywd ap Cil Coed, close friend of the queen's old suitor, Gwawl ap Clud. The enchanter had enslaved his royal prisoners, making Rhiannon pull his wagons in his horses' place and Pryderi carry the great beams that made fast his gates. Meanwhile, he continued his persecution of the land of Wales: as fast as Manawydan and Cigfa could cultivate the earth their crops were carried off and eaten by a plague of marauding mice that he had sent.

Driven almost to distraction, Manawydan chased the tiny terrors back and forth, but could never catch any – until one day he saw one that was bigger and more lumbering than the rest. Seizing it by the tail, he discovered it was Llywd's wife, encumbered by the fact that she was well advanced in pregnancy. Manawydan was able to hold her hostage: not until Pryderi and Rhiannon were released and Wales restored to its full fertility and populousness, with the promise of a lasting truce, did he agree to give his opponent back his wife. Once again, Gwenaby became a beautiful woman.

The Tale of Taliesin

One of Welsh tradition's most famous figures, the other notable survivor of the great battle in Ireland between Bendigeidfran and his forces and Matholwch over Branwen was Taliesin, now most celebrated as his country's bard. Taliesin arguably occupies the role in Wales that in Irish myth is divided between Fionn mac Cumhaill and his son Oisín. For, this warlike cameo apart, Taliesin's reputation rests on the *Book of Taliesin*, an eleventh-century collection of older poems that may or may not have been written by the same author, who in his (or her?) turn may or may not have been Taliesin. The sheer variety of these poems is impressive. They include weird narratives like the *Preiddeu Annwfn* ("Spoils of Annwn"), a renowned account of King Arthur's journey to the Otherworld, and the extraordinary *Cad Goddeu* (or "Battle of Trees"), in which the enchanter Gwydion fab Dôn mobilizes a whole forest by turning its trees into soldiers. But there are also love lyrics, elegies, philosophical meditations and even hymns.

Such evidence as there is for Taliesin's existence (and there *is* some, incidentally, however much his story may have grown in centuries of retelling) suggests that he wasn't Welsh at all. On the contrary, he appears to have been born and bred in what we would now think of as the north of England. Like Britain's Celtic inheritance as a whole, however, his memory was gradually erased in the Anglo-Saxon realm: it endured in Wales only by default. No

OEDIPAL UPSET

It seems odd to us as modern readers that Pryderi should have played so proactive a part in managing his mother's marital destiny – a disturbing twist on an already unsettling Oedipal myth. That both plunge their hands into a womblike golden bowl before being frozen perhaps points to the forbidden closeness theirs is seen to represent. Some approximation of a normal patriarchal service is restored, however, by the fact that mother and son are both finally delivered through the power of an older father figure, Manawydan.

THE SHEER VARIETY OF THESE POEMS IS IMPRESSIVE.

matter – his influence in that country was to be both powerful and profound. The legendary Taliesin resembled Fionn, not just in his military prowess (however scantily chronicled this was) but in his possession of all knowledge

HE WAS HIDEOUS, THE UGLIEST BEING IN THE WORLD.

by strange magical powers. In place of the Salmon-of-Knowledge story, a young boy named Gwion, just 13 years old, is said to have been walking past the mouth of the cave where the foul witch Ceridwen was cooking up a cauldron of special stew for her son Afaggdu. He was hideous – the ugliest being in the world – but his mother had decided that if he couldn't have looks, he could at least have compensating brains. Hence this magic concoction that, Ceridwen tiring (the cauldron had been bubbling away for over a year), she asked the passing boy to stir for a while: like Fionn's salmon, the stew spat up at him and he instinctively sucked his fingers.

BELOW: Overrun by the sea in mythic times, the lost land of Cantre'r Gwaelod is commemorated in a mosaic at Borth, Ceredigion.

When the witch became aware of what had happened and understood that all her months of toil and trouble for her son

LEFT: **For Taliesin in Wales, as for Fionn mac Cumhaill in Ireland, a cooking mishap meant a world of wisdom.**

had been completely wasted, she flew at Gwion in an explosive fit of rage. The teenager fled, transforming himself into a hare for speed. When she became a hound to chase him, he plunged into a river and became a fish – only to hear Ceridwen, now an otter, behind him in hot pursuit. Leaping clear of the surface, he became a bird only to find a falcon stooping to smash him out of the sky. Just in time he turned himself into a tiny seed. If he thought he'd escape detection this way, however, Gwion was sadly mistaken. Ceridwen, now a chicken, pecked him up and swallowed him.

A witch – and thus a woman – once more, Ceridwen carried on with her life and then, a few weeks later, realized that she was unaccountably with child. She immediately understood what had happened. This could only be the boy who had taken her son's stew – with all the knowledge in the world. There'd be no escaping for the meddler now, she resolved. No sooner was he born than she would kill him.

When he was eventually born, however, unwonted instincts took her over: she couldn't actually do this tiny mite to death. Instead, she tied him into a sack and tossed it into the sea, where, carried far away by the rushing current, it was found a few days later by Elphyn, a young prince of the House of Dyfed. Calling the child inside it "Taliesin" ("shining brow"), he brought him up as his foster son – like so many other misplaced children in Celtic myth. The rest is history – or, rather, it isn't really, though: like so much of Celtic myth, the tale of Taliesin does to some extent partake of truth.

OPPOSITE: **Taliesin's monument overlooks Llyn Geirionydd, northwest Wales, on whose banks the bard was reputed to have lived.**

A SYMBOLIC SAVIOUR

Taliesin's own account of his origins – in the book that bears his name – hints intriguingly at parallels between his story and that of Mabon and other foundling heroes. "I first grew to handsomeness", his poem says,

> Purified and formed in the hall of Ceridwen.
> Small and insignificant as I seemed,
> I grew to greatness in her vast sanctuary.

> In that prison
> I was inspired with understanding,
> Learned life's laws through wordless lessons.

His confinement in the witch's womb recalls that of Mabon in his deep dungeon. Equipped in his imprisonment with the experience and insight man will need to survive in the world, he becomes not just a poet but a deliverer – a status that can as easily be imagined in Christian as in pagan terms. Like Mabon before him, he's symbolically reborn as well – although this doesn't come with his birth but later, after days at sea, when Elphyn frees him from the sack Ceridwen had tied him in, at which point, renamed "Taliesin", he's ready to become his people's bard. (Of course, the sack in which a nation's wisdom is tied up tight also recalls the crane-skin "Treasure-Bag" of the Irish *Fianna*.

5

"TO THE WILDS!"

Ever more remote from its ancient origins, Celtic myth became increasingly polarized between the "high" and literary and the "low" and folkloric; between the court on the one hand and the cottage on the other.

Much inspired by the *Mabinogion*, Alfred, Lord Tennyson brought Celtic myth to arguably its widest ever audience when he published his poetic *Idylls of the King* through the 1870s and 80s. These Arthurian romances reimagined medieval – and much older – narratives for a modernity that envied what it thought of as the simplicity, the stateliness, the emotional sincerity and social stability of former times. But if Tennyson's wanderings in the world of Celtic myth were conservative in their origin, they were self-aware enough to sense the limitations of nostalgia; the challenge necessarily represented by changing times. In "Geraint and Enid" – directly drawn from the *Mabinogion* – he arguably wrote an epitaph for the entire Arthurian ideal.

OPPOSITE: Geraint sets off into the wilderness with Enid, his loving – but now spurned – wife.

A Knight Disarmed

Geraint was one of Arthur's boldest knights, renowned for his skill at arms and his courage in the field of battle. He was in the midst of one such warlike quest when he met Enid – her family gave him food, shelter and new armour when he needed it. There was no doubt that Geraint was blessed in her: Enid wasn't just dazzling and dizzying in her beauty, but she surpassed all other women in her wifely love. Such was her devotion, though, that his comrades came to feel that Geraint had been neglecting his knightly duties, comfortable as he was at home with Enid. So

BELOW: Domestic bliss – but is it also the corruption of a manly character? The story of Geraint aired such anxieties.

much so that he became an object, first of scorn and then, ultimately, of real contempt: he'd grown soft and given up his manhood, it was said. These whisperings reached Enid who, distraught, broke down in distress one night when she believed herself alone, bewailing the damage she appeared to have done to her husband's reputation. Geraint, outside her chamber door, half-hearing her lamentations and taking them for an admission of infidelity, felt furious alike with himself and with his wife. He would, he resolved, ride out into the world and win back the knightly reputation that had been so hard won; by his heroic deeds now he would recover the respect he'd lost. Geraint gave orders that his wife was to go with him. Disgraced as she was, however, she had to ride a little way ahead and not address a word to him, until she had at last made full amends for her supposed offences.

"And forth they rode, but scarce three paces on,
When crying out, 'Effeminate as I am,
I will not fight my way with gilded arms,
All shall be iron'; he loosed a mighty purse,
Hung at his belt, and hurled it toward the squire.
So the last sight that Enid had of home
Was all the marble threshold flashing, strown
With gold and scattered coinage, and the squire
Chafing his shoulder: then he cried again,
'To the wilds!'"

BELOW: Though the *Mabinogion* has Enid riding ahead of her angry husband, modern artists intuitively saw her trailing in the rear.

No Victorian reader would have been in much doubt as to the moral of the story: Geraint was a man emasculated by the power of woman's sexuality and by the restrictions of her domestic sphere. This might have been an age in which the bourgeois family was held up as an ideal, and the loyal and loving wife was lauded as the "Angel in the House". Even so, there was a paradox: how was the patriarch to prove his manly mettle when he was walking in the park with his family on a fine summer's afternoon, sitting round the fireside with them on a winter's evening, or working long days in an office to finance the whole thing? Geraint's resolve to reject "gold", money and the "marble" of an over-opulent and over-cosy home and instead to set out into the world and make his way, a man of "iron", may be read as a rebellion against a Victorian domesticity and an everyday routine of bourgeois life in which (at least apparently) woman reigned.

Romance in Revolt

But Geraint's words might be read in other ways as well: as, for instance, a reflection of real (if scarcely acknowledged) personal unease on Tennyson's part as an unprecedentedly popular Poet Laureate, a favourite of the British establishment and one of the country's comfortable and conformist middle class. Or even, perhaps, as a literary rejection of the Arthurian romance and what it was in danger of becoming. Granted, the Pre-Raphaelite painters and poets – not least the Marxist William Morris (and Tennyson himself in some of his earlier works) – had found Arthurian myths and their imagery a fertile field in which to explore quite daring and transgressive thoughts and feelings on everything from social organization to sexual desire. Lancelot's

adulterous love for Queen Guinevere – Arthur's wife – was (to take just one example) as much an affront to nineteenth-century family values as it had ever been to the medieval romancers' feudal code. This was a case of Celtic mythology doing in the modern day what it had done in its most distant past – tracing and testing society's deepest taboos.

Latterly, though – and not least in the other poems of Tennyson's *Idylls of the King* – this experimentation had given way to a more straightforward and uncritical conservative nostalgia. In this respect, perhaps, the Arthurian genre had run its course, come to a settled truce with the social values it found in the society around it. While it has maintained its popularity up to a point since then (and derivative "mythopoeic" works like Tolkien's have done much more), it has done so mainly by setting out into "the wilds" of fantasy. Or of playful parody, like T.H. White's.

The Night Shepherd

The *Bugul Noz* or "Night Shepherd" roams the woods and copses of Brittany by night, looking after the wild animals of the forest (hence his shepherd's title) and never showing his face by the light of day. If his presence is evidenced at all, it is by the loud and scary screams he occasionally emits – although, horrible as they are, these are benevolent in their intent. For the Bugul Noz is unbelievably – very likely unbearably – ugly, his visage so unimaginably hideous that a human who chanced upon him might quite easily drop dead from fright. Only on Halloween, when the Breton villagers themselves come out in all manner of ugly and outrageous guise, does he dare emerge from his hiding place deep in the woods.

THE SECRET COMMONWEALTH

"Every age hath some secret left for its discovery", wrote Robert Kirk, a Scottish clergyman, in 1691. For his own age (which was, we should remember, on the cusp of the "Scottish Enlightenment") this was "the nature and actions of the subterranean (and for the most part) invisible people, heretofore going under the name of elves, fauns and fairies." His book, *The Secret Commonwealth*, was a serious study of what we would now regard as a ridiculous non-subject. Intriguingly, though, Kirk's researches were supported by the Anglo-Irish philosopher, chemist and physicist Robert Boyle (*right*) – and this was a methodological thumbs-up that was well worth having. For while Boyle may be most famous for his law governing the relation of volume to pressure in gases, he is also widely credited with having helped to introduce a rigorous, experimental approach to modern science.

There does seem to have been some real belief in fairies on the part of ordinary Scottish people – especially, as might be expected, in the rural areas. Such stories certainly kept cropping up. The seventeenth-century "Fairy Boy of Leith" – just ten years old – told officials that, every Thursday night, he went deep down into the heart of Edinburgh's Calton Hill through an imposing set of gates (which were, however, invisible to other people) to play his drum amid scenes of fairy dancing and revelry. At around the same time, one Johnny Williamson – the "Boy of Borgue" – claimed to have many times descended into a bank of earth outside his Dumfries and Galloway village where he'd stay with the fairies – sometimes for days on end.

Even when Scots country people didn't actively believe in the existence of this "secret commonwealth", they sometimes seem to have liked to err on the side of caution. In the early nineteenth century, for example, one farmer, Alexander Simpson of Winchburgh, West Lothian, was keeping a corner of every field uncultivated as the Devil's share or "Guidman's Croft". Within a few decades, that same farmer's grandson James Young Simpson would be pioneering the anaesthetic use of chloroform.

From Faith to Folklore

Celtic legend more generally has endured mainly in "the wilds" in recent times. Not that this should surprise us: as we've seen, the culture of the Celts was banished to western Europe's margins as long ago as Roman times. There it has survived for the most part as "folklore" – a body of beliefs handed down the generations through the oral tradition. Or of half-beliefs, for few today are likely to credit the existence of the Irish *Sídhe* or Scottish *Sleagh Maith* ("Good People") as factually and objectively existing in the way that Dublin, the Forth Bridge, cars and NATO plainly do – or even in the way they may regard their religious faith. But half a belief may be enough – it has certainly been sufficient to see the folkloric traditions of Europe's "Celtic Fringe" endure as at least an imaginative influence in the modern consciousness. A "soft" presence, possibly, and yet a real one.

FOLKLORIC TRADITIONS ENDURE AS AN IMAGINATIVE INFLUENCE.

Scary Stories

For the most part, though, the Celtic myths have bequeathed a body of story and a stock of imagery. Mythic monsters, giants, fairies, enchanters and warrior heroes have haunted the modern consciousness, even where they haven't walked the Earth. Robert Burns' classic Scottish poem *Tam o' Shanter* (1791) makes no great claims to seriousness, but it draws upon what was clearly still a very vibrant, living tradition of story and of song.

BELOW: In Burns' *Tam o' Shanter*, the fairy folk were no longer frightening but a source of raucous, slightly risqué, fun.

Other representatives of that tradition still endure, such as the Selkie, a mysterious mythic creature that takes the shape of a seal for his or her life at sea but can come ashore at will, shedding its skin, to assume the form of a (breathtakingly beautiful) man or woman. In many Scottish stories, male Selkies seduce vulnerable women (often those whose human husbands have been lost at sea), although there are tales, too, of mortal men stealing female Selkies' sealskins so they have to stay on shore with them as wives. The legend underlines the liminal character of the seacoast as a threshold capable of being crossed in both directions. More straightforwardly brutal, the Kelpie is a kind of spirit-horse, said to lurk in Scotland's lochs and river pools. It, too, can take on human shape, although when it does so it keeps its horse's hooves. The Kelpie drags unwary travellers down into the deep and eats them up.

THE KELPIE DRAGS UNWARY TRAVELLERS DOWN INTO THE DEEP.

The Morgens of Welsh and Breton myth are rather more like the sirens of classical tradition: beautiful but deadly temptresses who lure seafarers to their doom. In Breton culture, this category

BELOW: **A wayfarer is startled by a hideously comic-looking Kelpie: Celtic folklore became an aspect of folk humour.**

A group of Korrigans make (potentially lethal) mischief for a traveller atop a Breton cliff.

overlaps with that of the Korrigan, a spirit that may be anywhere on the spectrum between mildly mischievous and downright evil, and that tends to be associated with water. They may be seen at night on the banks of springs or streams. (In the Breton song "Ar Rannou", collected in 1839 but almost certainly a great deal older, a druid describes nine Korrigans "dancing round a fountain, with flowers in the hair and wearing gowns of white linen, by the radiance of the full moon.") In other, more lurid and maybe more literary accounts, Korrigans live in the water itself and float enticingly just offshore, tossing their golden tresses, their naked bodies a-shimmer in the rippling starlight. Bewitched by desire, the mortal man passing by on the bank above can't

Nuberu, Sender of Storms

Springing up in a matter of moments, and ripping out of the northwest to strike the coast of Cantabria, Asturias and Galicia, the Galerna sends Spanish fishing vessels scurrying for port. So it has done for centuries, ever since the time when Celtiberian druids attributed these sudden storms to the wrath of Nuberu. An Iberian take on Taranis, the Gallic god of thunder, Nuberu has endured, albeit now demoted to a folkloric, semi-comic status as a luxuriantly bearded old man dressed head-to-foot in goatskin clothing.

Capricious as his anger is, Nuberu can be kind as well: he's often shown seated on a cloud as the bringer of vital rain. The story goes that he originally arrived in Spain seated astride a cloud but then slipped off and tumbled down to Earth. There he was rescued by an Asturian peasant, since which time he has helped to water the region's crops. There's no getting round his temper, though: he's easily offended, and quick to send the sort of torrential rainstorms, flash floods and lightning bolts that can make meteorological life in northwest Spain so scary at times.

resist reaching out to touch them: inevitably, he tumbles in and is dragged down to the bottom where he quickly drowns. The Korrigan can claim another victim; another victory for an Otherworld that in this view is essentially and invariably malicious.

The Korrigan's equivalent in Cornish tradition is the Korrik – although this is conventionally translated as "gnome", making it one of several similar spirit types to be found in Cornwall. The Bucca seems (although there's no real consensus) to inhabit the nocturnal countryside; the Knocker to be an inhabitant of the underworld – which of course a great many Cornishmen visited daily in their work as miners. Knockers made mischief for them, undoing their work or stealing their food and drink, although they don't seem to have been regarded as malevolent in any deeper way. Indeed, the "knocking" for which they were named seems to have been the banging in the walls and the creaking of the timber props that often heralded a roof-fall – ultimately, the Knockers were lifesavers.

These Cornish creatures are all less like the Breton water-sprite than the Irish Leprechaun. That spirit is hard to make out satisfactorily through the fog of twee sentimentality on the one hand and Anglo-American ethnic stereotyping on the other. Media depictions of the Leprechaun since the nineteenth century have tended to show a striking resemblance to representations of the immigrant Irishman himself, as a leering rogue, a combative thug or a cheery clown. A culturally and politically influenced version, then, of the same transition from serious (sometimes

OPPOSITE: Half-engaging, half-alarming, Shakespeare's mischievous fairy Puck shows clearly how early-modern attitudes were changing.

A DEMANDING MOTHER

The Poor Old Woman, said the Irish songs, had "four beautiful green fields" (the island's provinces), but there were "strangers in the kitchen" – English occupiers. That same old woman has had many guises, among them the Sean-Bhean bhocht (or Shan Van Vocht) of the United Irishmen's 1798 rebellion – left badly in the lurch when promised French assistance failed to materialize. She reappeared in later times of nationalist crisis as Cathleen ni Houlihan. No young beauty but a broken-down old crone, weak and impoverished – and helpless without the sacrifices of her sons – she symbolized an Irish nation that had to fight to win back what had been lost. A comparatively modern, political (and frankly propagandistic) creation, this personification nevertheless recognizably harked back to much more ancient archetypes. Like the Morrigan, she's a mother figure, yet an anything-but-cuddly, brutally exacting one, demanding her children's blood – however noble her ultimate cause may be.

sinister) spirit-being to playful, essentially engaging fairy-folk of popular English culture. As far removed as Tinker Bell in J.M. Barrie's 1904 play *Peter Pan* may seem from the ancient Celtic spirits, it still seems significant that her creator was a Scot, while the fairies of Shakespeare's *A Midsummer Night's Dream* (c. 1595) are widely assumed to draw on a semi-submerged (and ultimately Celtic) English folk tradition. Shakespeare's place is pivotal, indeed: while fairies like Mustardseed, Moth and Peaseblossom are uncomplicatedly cute and unthreatening, Puck (or "Robin Goodfellow") is more ambivalent – witty, but with a distinctly dark, sadistic streak. He wouldn't have been out of place in a much older and more disturbing Celtic legend.

ABOVE: **Washerwomen make strange sirens, perhaps, but Brittany's Kannerezed Noz never had too much trouble luring their victims to their fate.**

Les Lavandières

In Breton tradition, the *Kannerezed Noz* ("Night Washerwomen") are seen in a group of three by moonlit riversides, washing the shrouds for those who are about to die. Mortal travellers passing by may be asked to lend a hand, but woe betide them if they let their obliging instincts get the better of their sense of caution. Stories abound of the women abruptly banding together to bundle their unwary victim into the shroud he's helping with. Never, it goes without saying, to be seen again.

Similar spirits are to be found in the traditions both of Scotland and of Ireland: as a trio, they recall the threefold Morrigna. In fact, if we're to believe the myths, the Breton night is swarming with spirits: lost souls like the

THE BRETON NIGHT IS SWARMING WITH SPIRITS.

bugel-noz ("night child") and the *skrijerez-noz* ("night-screecher"). Like the Irish banshee, the skrijerez-noz screams in anguish in anticipation of a dear one's death: both these spirits are associated with the cry of the ghostly-white barn or "screech" owl.

Lost Countries, Sunken Cities

Dolly Pentreath died in 1777: as the monument at her graveside in Paul, high up on the hillside behind Mousehole harbour, says, she was believed to be "one of the last speakers of the Cornish language". That was almost a quarter of a millennium ago. Even now, Cornwall is much more than a county, though, like so much of Europe's Celtic fringe, it struggles to keep its end up, both culturally and economically. It is much the same story across the sea in La Cornuaille in France's Maine-et-Loire, its Celtic patrimony more a matter of vague pride than of political reality.

But then Celtic mythology always had that "dying fall", that suggestion of sadness, of loss, of melancholy. The story of the Lost City of Ys is a case in point. Some say it stands to this day, beneath the water's of Brittany's Baie de Douarnenez. In some accounts, it was built below the level of the sea to start with by Cornuaille's King Gralon: high retaining walls protected it from the surrounding waves and special gates let shipping come and go. In others, Ys was built on a coastal site and only then enveloped by the waters: either way, the story is typically Celtic in its suggestion of liminality, of the crossing over of two different worlds and of the mysterious possibilities to be found beneath the surfaces of things.

AN UNRELIABLE GUIDE

Yan-gant-y-tan, or (roughly) "Johnny-with-the-Fire", is a late-night wanderer in the forests of Finistère in the far west of Brittany – a little like the Will-o'-the-wisp of other European cultures. The fingers of his right hand end in tallow candles whose glow can lead unwary travellers astray. Definitely a demonic being, he has nevertheless been known to help wayfarers out of tight spots, giving them lamps to light their way – moral consistency was never particularly a feature of the Celtic spirit.

BELOW: The sign is self-explanatory, but its full significance maybe less so: Dolly's death marked the passing of "Celtic Cornwall".

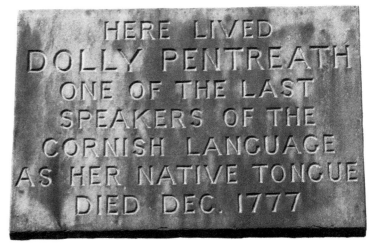

HERE LIVED
DOLLY PENTREATH
ONE OF THE LAST
SPEAKERS OF THE
CORNISH LANGUAGE
AS HER NATIVE TONGUE
DIED DEC. 1777

6

THE CELTIC LEGACY

Celtic legend can feel impossibly remote for today's reader, its meanings obscure and its imagery elusive. In its sheer lyricism and longing, though, it keeps compelling our attention, maintaining an irresistible hold over the modern mind.

There does seem to have been an Iron Age settlement at Tintagel, on the northern coast of Cornwall, so the place's Celtic credentials are unimpeachable. But the archeological evidence doesn't run to much more than a few fragments of broken pottery. Spectacularly situated on a storm-swept clifftop, Tintagel Castle is too romantic to be true – not surprisingly, since the structure we see today is largely a nineteenth-century, neo-Arthurian confection. And that, it might be said, is the Celtic Legacy in a nutshell: a scant reality underlying a world of resonance.

Does that discredit the whole heritage? Yes and no. Yes, if we're going to imagine that a Victorian fake ruin faithfully

OPPOSITE: **Its ruined structure as striking as its situation is sublime, Tintagel Castle clings to a clifftop on Cornwall's coast.**

reflects an Iron Age reality; no, if we're prepared to accept that such a reality might be reimagined – and quite legitimately – over time. As we've seen, the illiteracy the Celts themselves elected placed them in a strange and problematic relation to ancient "history" from the very start: they have just about always had to be seen through others' eyes. Conversely, though, the absence of any more definitely delineated Celtic reality (like that of Greece or Rome) has arguably allowed them an imaginative – even, perhaps, a subconscious – presence in western culture.

There can be a reality in romance, moreover. Tintagel does figure in some of the old stories of Arthur's court: the king was actually conceived here, according to the *Historia Regum Britanniae*. It is also an important setting in the story of Tristan and Yseult, one of the most moving stories of doomed passion ever told. It is chiefly familiar nowadays from its thirteenth-century Middle High German rendering by Gottfried von Strassburg, by way of Richard Wagner's opera *Tristan und Isolde* (composed in the 1850s). In the Tristan legend, Tintagel is the seat not of Arthur but of King Mark of Cornwall. He sends his handsome young nephew Tristan off to Ireland to bring back his intended bride, the beautiful young princess Yseult. The two are attracted to one another: how could so lively and passionate a maiden and so dashing a young knight not be? But they know that the rules of loyalty and honour forbid their relationship. In the course of the sea voyage back, however, they accidentally take a love potion and fall head-over-heels for one another: by the time they make Tintagel they are ardent lovers. So much for King Mark's virgin bride. But the show of propriety must go on, the King kept in ignorance, and he and Yseult are duly wed. Tristan and Yseult's relationship – now what we might call an "affair" – continues.

BELOW: **King Arthur was treacherously killed at Slaughterbridge, Cornwall, in 537, it is said. Could this slab really mark the mythic ruler's grave?**

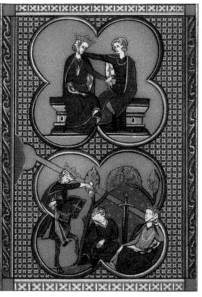

LEFT: The romance of Cligès (left) satirized the Tristan story's idealized adultery (right): here they confront each other on facing pages.

To coin a cliché, how can what feels so right be so wrong? The place of the potion has been pivotal, of course: the weight it is given in Von Strassburg's version of the story in particular allows the young lovers to pursue their passion without serious moral compromise. Umpteen different versions of the romance exist, and for the most part they end badly (with Tristan's death and often Yseult's too), but somehow it seems the sheer depth of their feeling has redeemed it. That

THE RULES OF LOYALTY AND HONOUR FORBID THEIR RELATIONSHIP.

was certainly the sense the first listeners to Wagner's treatment were left with as they went away reeling from the luxuriant lyricism of his opera's final Liebestod, "love death", aria, sung by the stricken Isolde over Tristan's corpse.

Wagnerian Warning

Wagner, it goes without saying, is as much a warning as an inspiration – ecstatically as his work evokes those imaginative reaches of the human heart and mind that transcend our ready comprehension. While it never does us any harm to be reminded of the limits of our conscious understanding, those who embrace irrationalism do tend quickly to leave normal decencies behind. Wagner's anti-Semitism was as squalid as his music was sublime;

ABOVE: **Richard Wagner created astonishing operas out of mythic material, but if they were intoxicating they were often toxic too.**

BELOW: **Wagner's *Parsifal* found dark and disturbing implications in the seeming chivalry of Arthurian myth.**

his operatic project clearly coopted ancient Celtic and Germanic myth as a means of sidestepping the normal conventions of modern historiography. Half a century or so later, Hitler and Himmler would need no encouragement to find in his work the basis of a new and essentially violent, racist domineering nationalism.

Another opera ultimately derived from a Celtic source, *Parsifal* (1882), a version of the Holy Grail legend, was to prove one of the most formative experiences in the early life of Joseph Goebbels. Its story sets King Arthur's Knights in general, and Sir Perceval in particular, in opposition to a dark anti-chivalric order led by Klingsor, duke and sorcerer – and a cipher, some felt, for the corrosive toxicity of the Jews in Wagner's eyes. The inference is by no means improbable, but it is worth bearing in mind as well that, along with Goebbels, great Jewish composers like Gustav Mahler were also to fall helplessly under *Parsifal*'s sway.

Others were to tap the Romantic "wildness" of the Celtic culture without going to Wagnerian extremes. The novels of Sir Walter Scott swept Europe, North America and much of the world beyond in the Victorian era, inspiring endless poems, plays and operas by other hands. Open as they are to the criticism of taking a stereotyping – and ultimately demeaning – view on "Scottishness", their most damaging legacy has been a certain amount of silly "tartanry" and some tasteless shortbread

tins. Scott was especially interesting in the way he harnessed the Celtic strand in modern Scottish culture as a way of lending more vividness and excitement to an established British culture that had arguably become a bit staid and stuffy. While Britain projected what we might nowadays call "hard power" with its Royal Navy and its conquering colonial armies, backed up by the economic might of the world's most advanced and prosperous industries, it won important "soft power" by promoting this more romantic and mysterious "Celtic" side. Queen Victoria's building of Balmoral Castle; the vogue for Scottish country dancing; kilted soldiers marching, sporrans swinging, behind skirling bagpipe bands … all added colour to Britain's image in the world outside.

ABOVE: **Sir Walter Scott's imaginative realization of Scotland's romantic possibilities helped give the Celtic idea a new lease of (after-)life.**

Condescending to the Celts

A more thoughtful nineteenth-century consideration is to be found in Matthew Arnold's essay, *The Study of Celtic Literature* (1866) – more thoughtful, but not necessarily deeper or more reliable. Arnold's view – that, essentially, the Celts had profoundly lyrical instincts but lacked the organizational skills to create greater or more lasting literature – neatly sums up wider English attitudes to the Irish, Scots and Welsh. Even early critics noted Arnold's lack of any actual knowledge of the languages whose heritage he was discussing – and that he didn't see this as any great handicap is significant in itself. Not until the 1900s would a critic (Adolphus William Ward) point out that, in such circumstances, Arnold's Olympian pronouncements represented "as adventurous an example of skating on the thin ice of criticism as anything to be found in our literature".

But the condescension implicit in Arnold's approach had been manifested much more disturbingly in England's reaction to the Irish Famine of the 1840s. The failure of the potato crop in 1845 (and subsequent years) had been directly caused by a blight, *Phytophthora infestans*. But the ravages of a famine that killed a million people and sent a million more into exile by emigrant ship (in the process blighting what remained of Ireland's Gaelic-

ABOVE: **For many in England, by a cruel irony, the Irish famine only underlined the childlike helplessness of the Celtic race.**

speaking Celtic culture) were the result in part of a view that the Irish were by their nature a rebellious and shiftless race, who should not be encouraged in their dependency. As the century wore on, and anger at landholding practices in Ireland continued, agrarian unrest at village level (and, on a wider stage, the actions of revolutionary groups like the Fenians) only confirmed Anglo-Saxons in their view that the Irish were at best hot-headed and at worst incorrigibly brutal and subhuman.

The view of Thomas Carlyle, a (self-hating?) Scot, that the Irishman existed in a state of "squalid apehood", seemed easy enough to defend in what was after all coming to be the golden age of "race theory". In the decades that followed, elaborately scientific-sounding theories were going to "demonstrate" the

RACE THEORY

With all its intellectual pretensions, the race theory by which so many in the nineteenth century set such store often now seems like so much old-fashioned prejudice tricked out in scientific-sounding terms. But then the converse could be true as well: while the use in colloquial English of the verb to "welsh" for the action of reneging on a bet or other agreement can be dated only as far back as the 1860s, it finds a foreshadowing in the much more soberly expressed and scholarly seeming observation of Giraldus Cambrensis (*right*), a Norman bishop based in twelfth-century Wales. The people there, he reports,

rarely keep their promises, for their minds are as fickle as their bodies are agile. It is very easy to persuade them to do something wrong, and just as easy to stop them once they have started. They are always quick to take action, and they are particularly stubborn when what they are doing is reprehensible. The only thing they really persist in is changing their minds ...

The suggestion that, with all their engaging innocence, a Celtic people might be lacking in that basic stability of mind that in "us" is seen as differentiating adults from young children is one of comparatively few things Anglo-Saxon culture has persisted in.

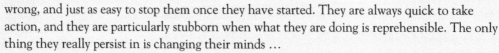

self-evident destiny of the white man to take up the "burden" of bringing government and order to the lives of all the various African and Asian nations. And, of course, the secret sickness that was represented by the Jews. Against such a background, the much gentler condescension felt by the most decent and compassionate Englishmen and -women towards the "Celtic" peoples, with their "native" lyricism and ingenuous good humour, barely seems to signify.

Emigration and Exile

The nineteenth century wasn't marked only by the rise of race theory and colonialism but by that of *laissez-faire* capitalism as well. Dogmatic free-market principles had helped underpin Britain's non-response to the Irish Famine, vastly exacerbating its impact both in the immediate and the longer term. The Celtic nations had for centuries been consigned to poorer lands on Europe's western margins: those lands were among the first to feel the effects of all the continent's economic crises. The torrent of emigrants across the Atlantic from Ireland was followed by streams from Galicia and Brittany.

More, of course, were to come from Scotland, where the "Highland Clearances" were hitting hard. As in Ireland, modern economic orthodoxies were wreaking havoc with ancient ways of life: after so many centuries, the traditional clan system was breaking down. This time, however, it wasn't an occupying English elite that was destroying the old Celtic culture: the old ways were being betrayed by the Highland chiefs themselves. Seduced by the prospect of private wealth and luxury into turning their territories over to sheep farming, they were soon evicting their tenants (formerly their clansmen and -women) in their thousands.

It is hardly surprising that the cultural output of the generations of Celtic writers and artists these times produced should have been so strongly characterized by its minor key. Galician poetry even had a word for this hallmark longing tone: *saudade*. "All is mute silence, sadness", wrote that country's greatest poet, Rosalía de Castro: "pain, where once reigned only contentment, joy". The absence of familiar voices; the

BELOW: **Brought up speaking Spanish, but electing to write in Galician, Rosalía de Castro (1837–85) set** *saudade* **into verse.**

emptiness of bereavement and of exile; an indescribable and all but unbearable nostalgia: these were the inheritance this period was to leave Galicia with. Writers across the Celtic fringe were to express much the same thought. As did those in what was coming to be an extensive diaspora: "Half of Galicia is on the outside", observes a character in one recent Galician novel, Manuel Rivas' *All is Silence* (2010).

BARDS AND BOUNDERS

Iolo Morganwg (or, as he was less memorably christened, Edward Williams) was Wales' answer to Scotland's James Macpherson. In every sense, for the first modern Welsh-language bard was at once a man of prodigious talent and a downright fraud, and it's very difficult to know which should remain uppermost of his memory. Many of the medieval manuscripts he "discovered" turned out after his death to have been forgeries, yet he arguably reinvented Welsh as a modern literary language.

The Ossian scandal had already broken when Williams/Morganwg made his way to London in the 1770s to join what was then a small but already growing Welsh language antiquarian and literary scene, but true enthusiasts refused to be discouraged. With fellow-members, Morganwg helped promote their country's first *eisteddfodau* in Wales itself – gatherings at which Welsh culture could be celebrated in musical performance, poetic declamation and dance. These helped pave the way for the first National Eisteddfod, held in Bala in 1789.

A worthy tradition, and yet one that by century's end was withering away. Ordinary Welshmen and -women felt little need to get involved. It seems to have been only when they felt they were under Saxon attack that the Welsh were galvanized to organize and come to the defence of their home country and its culture. The provocation came from an on the face of it improbable source: the *Reports of the Commissioners of Enquiry into the State of Education in Wales*, a government "Blue Book" (official publication, so called from the uniform colour of its cover) of 1847. But its author expressed himself in some decidedly unparliamentary language. Wales, he opined (or, rather, laid down the law, for he was setting out official government policy) was "a primitive backwater, ignorant and immoral"; Welsh-language "education" was positively holding the country back. English was now to be the medium of teaching: to encourage better practice in the years that followed, little signs reading "Welsh Not" were hung around the necks of children who lapsed into their native tongue. (In fairness, it should be stated that language wasn't Wales' only problem: the people's Nonconformist religious views can't have helped, as far as an Anglican officialdom was concerned. Ironically, their deeply Protestant views seem to have afflicted them just as badly and in much the same ways as Roman Catholicism did the peasantry of Ireland.) The so-called "Treachery of the Blue Books" seems to have done what Morganwg and his friends had failed to do: jumpstart a cultural renaissance in the land of Wales.

Rivas goes on to describe an old schoolhouse just outside the coastal village where his story is set: it seems to be "propped up, supported" by nature: "One of those ruins that wants to disappear but can't, which is bound, not cleft, by the ivy on the walls". That sense of inversion, of everything being inside out, of immediate reality being in some sense constructed by what's beyond it, of the country in some sense being constituted by its exiles, is common to all these nations and represents another continuity with the deeper Celtic past. Liminality, the criss-crossing of boundaries between one dimension and another, is once more at the aesthetic heart of things.

The Children of Lir

It is a thing about yearning, maybe, that makes the Celtic influence still thrill in the modern mind. To that extent Matthew Arnold was right: as patronizing as his view may have been; as profoundly unscholarly as his conclusions, it is certainly what we see as Celtic lyricism that arrests the imagination now. And there's no doubt that, whatever its achievements in everything from epic adventure to high comedy, Celtic mythology has often shown a wistful sadness that has particularly stirred the modern soul. One of the most moving myths in the whole heritage of Celtic legend is that of the Children of Lir. Their story starts with the figure of Bodb Derg. We met Bodb briefly in the story of the *Táin Bó Cuailnge*. As King of Munster he was the unfortunate employer of Rucht, whose war with rival pig-man Friuch was to cause such chaos. But he had a previous existence as a god, a son and successor to the Daghda as King of the *Tuatha Dé Danann*. But his authority was challenged by Lir, a lesser king, whose realm was in Westmeath. (Lir's name identifies him with Ler, an older maritime deity like the Welsh sea-god known as Llyr – although not it seems to the British Celtic king – and unhappy father – whose story was to be told by Shakespeare.) Keen to conciliate his enemy, Bodb Derg gave his daughter Aoibh to Lir in marriage. The match was happy and produced four children: a sister and a brother, Fionnuala and Aodh, and a pair of boy-twins, Fiachra and Conn.

BELOW: **Oisín Kelly's Children of Lir statue in Dublin's Garden of Remembrance commemorates those who died in Ireland's freedom struggle.**

Aoibh died, leaving an unhappy house. Eager to cheer his grandchildren and maintain his matrimonial connection with King Lir, Bodb Derg offered him Aoibh's younger sister, Aoife, to be his wife. Aoife's name meant "radiant with beauty", but while she lived up to it in looks her temperament was altogether darker. (She too appears in other myths – most notably as the warlike twin sister of Scáthach and sometime lover of Cú Chulainn, whose ill-fated son Connla she also bore.) For all her loveliness, she found it hard, confronted with a family whose father and children were so strongly bonded by their bereavement and by their longing for the wife and mother who was no longer there.

ABOVE: A whale, says one medieval myth, helped St Brendan and his party to celebrate mass safely far out at sea.

Banished with the Birds

Aoife's transition from beloved sister-in-law and aunt to jealous wife and "wicked stepmother" was swift and complete. Her marriage would be fine, she felt, if it weren't for those accursed children. Scheming obsessively to find some way to be rid of them, she finally decided that they would have to be done away with. One day, while she was travelling with them, taking them to Bodb's court for a visit to their grandfather, she asked the servant who was attending her to murder her stepchildren. When he recoiled in outrage, she flew into a temper and tried to kill them herself – but she too, enraged as she was, could not quite bring herself to do so. Still implacably vindictive, though, and resolved to have them out of her life for good, she turned them into swans and sent them off into the sky to fly with the birds. For 300 years, she commanded, they would have to dwell amid the waters and the reed beds of Lough Derravaragh, beside their father's castle in Westmeath. When that period was over, they would have to fly far to the north to spend 300 years on the Sea of Moyle, between Scotland's Kintyre and Ireland's Antrim coast. Finally, they would set out for the west to Sruwaddacon Bay, an extensive inlet of the coast of Co. Mayo. There (in what is still, appropriately, a bird and wildlife sanctuary), they would spend a further 300 years. Only then,

Aoife said, would they at last find their freedom on the offshore Isle of Inishglora. "Heaven's bell" would call them, she promised.

As chance (or God's grace) would have it, by that time, nine centuries later, this remote and rugged island was home to the hermitage of the great St Brendan. Chiefly famous for his epic voyage by hide-covered coracle across the North Atlantic to Iceland (or was it, some scholars have asked, even America?), Brendan was also important for his missionary work in his native Ireland. One morning, it is said, he was walking along the

> "HEAVEN'S BELL" WOULD CALL THEM, SHE PROMISED.

Inishglora strand when he saw four sad-looking swans in the waters just offshore: at that moment, the bell above his chapel rang. Abruptly the Children of Lir were released from Aoife's enchantment and once again restored to human form. Over 900 years old by now, of course, they were no longer "children" but living mummies: they promptly died, their bodies crumbling into dust. But this at least could be buried and prayed over, according to the new Christian rite that now prevailed in Ireland, so that they could be consigned to the earth in the hope of rest and resurrection.

Sleep of the Soul

In some versions of the story, the vehicle of their salvation is St Patrick, Ireland's patron. It scarcely matters: the important point, obviously, is that the children's deliverance from Aoife's spell is matched with Ireland's from paganism, from darkness and from sin. The plight of the swan-children has been symbolic of spiritual sleep. In the centuries that followed, patriotic Irishmen and -women were to feel that their country was asleep again, in what they felt was too passive a political posture towards the English. Hence the nationalist take on the Children of Lir story adopted by Romantic lyricist Thomas Moore in his "Song of Fionnula" (1811):

> Silent, oh Moyle, be the roar of thy water,
> Break not, ye breezes, your chain of repose,
> While, murmuring mournfully, Lir's lonely daughter
> Tells to the night-star her tale of woes.

When shall the swan, her death-note singing,
Sleep, with wings in darkness furl'd?
When will heav'n, its sweet bell ringing,
Call my spirit from this stormy world?
Sadly, oh Moyle, to thy winter-wave weeping,
Fate bids me languish long ages away;
Yet still in her darkness doth Erin lie sleeping,
Still doth the pure light its dawning delay.
When will that day-star, mildly springing,
Warm our isle with peace and love?
When will heav'n, its sweet bell ringing,
Call my spirit to the fields above?

The melody to this song is played by a busking harpist in a
Dublin street in James Joyce's tale "Two Gallants" (in *Dubliners*,
1914) – ironically, while said "gallants" are disdainfully
discussing some young "tart". The "darkness" in which Ireland
lies "sleeping" might be anything from colonialist oppression
to *petit bourgeois* philistinism, self-satisfied mediocrity and
the complacent boorishness represented by the young men's
comments about the girl. Ireland itself was a "stepmother", semi-
joked Joyce in the satirical poem *Gas from a Burner* (1912); in
Ulysses (1922), his protagonist Stephen Dedalus was to confess
that "history is a nightmare from which I am trying to awake".

Celtic Swansong

For W.B. Yeats, walking in the grounds of Coole Park, Co.
Galway, the sight of a flock of swans prompted thoughts of
a natural beauty that persists despite the ups and downs of
human life, with its cycles of birth and death; lost love; the
disappearance of youth and its illusions; the inexorable march of
time. Every autumn, he muses, he comes to Coole, walks by this
"brimming water", which "mirrors a still sky", and sees what seem
to be the exact same swans, unchanged by time:
    I have looked upon those brilliant creatures,
    And now my heart is sore.
    All's changed since I, hearing at twilight,
    The first time on this shore,

The bell-beat of their wings above my head,
Trod with a lighter tread.

Unwearied still, lover by lover,
They paddle in the cold
Companionable streams or climb the air;
Their hearts have not grown old;
Passion or conquest, wander where they will,
Attend upon them still.
("The Wild Swans at Coole", 1917)

Lady Augusta Gregory, Yeats' friend (and, as the owner of Coole
Park, his hostess), had herself translated many Irish myths into
English, including her version of "The Fate of the Children of
Lir" in 1905. Although never explicitly referenced, the legend
nudges at the back of our minds while we read this poem. Perhaps
this, in the end, is the part that Celtic legends play in our
modern consciousness – and it is a stronger part, paradoxically,
than it would be were it more overt. Just as the Celts cast a
longer shadow than they would, perhaps, if we knew more about
them; and just as their legends haunt us the more powerfully for
so often being incomplete, inchoate, inconsistent – and utterly
incomprehensible at times. Celtic mythology comes to us as
through a mist, in half-glimpsed forms and glancing images that
only makes them resonate the more insistently in our minds. In
that respect, it could hardly be more modern.

BELOW: Swans (or
spirits?) glide across the
water in Coole Park.
Legends like those of
the Celts open up a
marvellous and magical
perspective on the
world.

GLOSSARY

Ailill mac Máta King of Connacht and the husband of queen Medb.

Beltane The May Day festival that traditionally marked the start of summer.

Connacht The northwestern province of Ireland, extending roughly from what's now Galway to Co. Sligo.

Cú Chulainn Born Sétanta, the "Hound of Chulainn" was the great Ulster hero of the *Táin bo Cuailgne*.

Culhwch The main protagonist in the story *Culhwch and Olwen*, he pursues the hand of Olwen as a result of a curse put on him by his stepmother.

Dál Riata A Celtic kingdom which, around the middle of the first millennium AD, spanned the strait between northeastern Ulster and southwestern Scotland.

Dindshenchas An old Irish text describing the mythic origins of a particular place name.

Donn Cuailnge The Brown Bull of Cooley was an extremely fertile stud bull over whom the *Táin Bó Cúailnge* (Cattle Raid of Cooley) was fought.

Epona Gaulish horse goddess, later adopted by the Romans.

Fianna The band of outlaw warriors led by Chumaill, and then by his son Fionn.

Finnegas The wise druid who inadvertently introduced Fionn mac Cumaill to the Salmon of Knowledge.

Fionn mac Cumhaill Mythic Irish hero, subject of the Fenian Cycle and an important figure in Scottish myth as well. Later he came to be seen as a semi-comic giant.

Galicia The ancient Celtic territory of northwest Spain. (Though there's another one – also supposedly settled by Celts – along the border between Poland and the Ukraine.)

Hallstatt An archaeological site in the Austrian Alps which has given its name to the early Celtic period (c. 8–600 BC).

La Tène An archaeological site in Switzerland whose name has been given to the whole highly-ornamental artistic style of the later Celts.

Lebor Gabála Érenn The "Book of Invasions" – a strongly mythic "history" of Ireland, first written in the eleventh century.

Lughnasadh A festival celebrating the sun, and the start of the harvest season.

Mabinogion The main collection of Welsh Celtic myth, assembled in the fourteenth century, though written down during the twelfth – and passed down orally for hundreds of years before.

Medb The beautiful but ruthless Queen of Connacht in the *Táin*.

Munster The southwestern part of Ireland, extending roughly from what's now Co. Clare to Co. Cork.

Oisín Son of Fionn mac Cumhaill, celebrated as Ireland's greatest bard.

Olwen Daughter of Ysbaddaden, she was the fairest maiden in Wales and pursued by Culhwch.

Oppidum Name given by the Romans to the type of fortified Celtic town they found in Gaul.

Pryderi Prince of Dyfed, a major hero of the Welsh mythic sequence, the *Mabinogion*.

Pwyll King of Dyfed (mid-Welsh kingdom) in the *Mabinogion*. Pryderi's father.

Rhiannon Wife to Pwyll, mother of Prince Pryderi, and overall a central mother-figure, in Welsh myth.

Samhain The Celtic festival of darkness, death and winter, celebrated at the end of October (like the later Halloween).

Sídhe In Irish tradition, the fairy folk – formerly seen as deities. (The word may also be used for the mounds they supposedly live in.)

Táin Bó Cúailnge "The Cattle Raid of Cooley": an ancient Irish epic describing the wars between Ulster and Connacht. Thought to have first been written down in the twelfth century, though set over a thousand years before.

Taliesin A famous warrior, and Wales' most important bard.

Tuatha Dé Danann Literally, the "Tribe of Danu", this was the name given to the old deities of Celtic Ireland.

Ulster The northernmost province of Ireland, extending from Donegal in the west to Antrim in the east.

Ysbaddaden The Giant King, father of Olwen.

INDEX

PICTURE CREDITS

AKG Images: 59

Alamy: 8 (North Wind), 13 (Interfoto), 15 (Imagebroker), 20 (Art Archive), 21 (North Wind), 23 (Interfoto), 24 (Yolanda Perera Sanchez), 27 (Kevin George), 32 (Ancient Art & Architecture Collection), 33 (North Wind), 35 (Peter Wheeler), 38 (QED Images), 40 (Art Archive), 48 (Art Archive), 55 (David Lyons), 56 (Travelib Ireland), 60 (Chronicle), 62 (Robert Malone), 63 (Scienceireland.com/Christopher Hill), 65 (Doug Houghton), 66 (Ancient Art & Architecture Collection), 67 (Alain Le Garmseur 'The Troubles Archive'), 70 (John Warburton-Lee), 72 (Chronicle), 76 (Chronicle), 85 (Fine Art), 89 (David Lyons), 92 (MOB Images), 94 (Holmes Garden Photos), 96 (North Wind), 97 (Radharc Images), 100 (Steppenwolf), 103 (David Lyons), 106 (Elizabeth Leyden), 110 (Jack Maguire), 116 (Classic Image), 120 (Pictorial Press), 122 (Chronicle), 123 (Design Pics Inc), 124 (AF Fotografie), 125 (J Orr), 127 (De Luan), 128 (Mike Rex), 133 (Chronicle), 143l (Lebrecht Music & Arts Photo Library), 138 (AMC), 146 (Cameron Cormack), 150 (Alwyn Jones), 152 (Chronicle), 154 (Stuart Walker), 156 (Interfoto), 159 (Jeff Morgan), 163 (Jeff Morgan), 164 (Art Archive), 165 (Prisma Archivo), 172 (Mick Sharp), 186 (Keith Morris), 188 (Ange), 190 (Newberry Library), 192 (Chronicle), 194 (Newberry Library), 195 (Print Collector), 196 (Print Collector), 199 (North Wind), 202 (Hemis), 203 (Roger Cracknell), 204 (Michael Wills), 206 (Celtic Collection – Homer Sykes), 207 (Falkensteinphoto), 209 (GL Archive), 210t (Print Collector), 210b (Classic Image), 211 (Pictorial Press), 212 (Graham Bell), 213 (Donal Murphy Photography), 217 (Alain Le Garmseur)

Alamy/Heritage Image Partnership: 6, 16, 18b, 19, 31, 44/45, 47, 68, 69, 77, 104, 129, 158, 208t

Alamy/Ivy Close Images: 57, 75, 87, 108, 126, 132, 183, 193

Alamy/Mary Evans Picture Library: 51, 81, 90, 93, 134r, 140, 162, 173, 197, 201

Bridgeman Art Library: 175 (Stapleton Collection), 182, 187

Corbis: 26 (Leemage)

Depositphotos: 10 (Ramonespelt1), 43 (JoannElle), 50 (MardyM), 95 (Design Pics Inc), 169 (Spumador)

Dreamstime: 9 (Gazzag), 28 (Daniel M. Cisilino), 36 (Pattdug), 58 (Ihorga), 79 (St Bernard Studio), 130/131 (Lokono), 145 (Quadrio)

Fotolia: 22 (Antonio Alcobendas), 30 (Erica Guilane-Nachez), 37 (Legabatch), 41 (Erica Guilane-Nachez), 64 (Erica Guilane-Nachez), 148 (Vanderwolf Images)

Getty Images: 17 (Hulton), 18t (De Agostini), 86 (IIC/Axiom), 180 (Leemage), 208b (Ullstein Bild), 214 (De Agostini)

iStock: 153 (Madmickandmo), 181 (Froggery)

Mary Evans Picture Library: 52, 54 (Arthur Rackham Collection), 82, 83, 84, 98, 102, 113, 114 (Historic England), 131 (Arthur Rackham Collection), 141 (Arthur Rackham Collection), 142 (Arthur Rackham Collection), 167 (Illustrated London News), 176, 198

Topfoto: 101, 137, 178, 184 (Fortean)